Aldo Agostinelli Silvio Meazza

PEOPLE ARE MEDIA

Digital business in the selfie era

Table of contents

Preface

By **Marco Montemagno**

A blunt review of some world-changing technological breakthroughs and their sociological consequences, this book will give you a wealth of thoughtful hints if you wish to learn about the moment in history we're going through: our increasingly 'social' society, its positive and negative inferences and the countless nuances in between.

This book covers a lot of things: Industry 4.0, big data, Blockchains, social media, the Internet of Things, and the way these innovations are impacting our everyday life and changing history. Above all, this book is a reminder – coming from two professionals who've been dealing with digital technologies for 25 years – that we should always use our best judgment.

The silver thread is always us, the people: we're both the *agents* of change and the *media* that experience, tell about and share such change.

Even the tiniest and seemingly insignificant device update brings about a revolution of some kind. Just think about the rear camera on our smartphones. Until recently, we would take pictures of places, people or scenes that were outside of us, and our focus was outward-looking. Now we take selfies, we're the undisputed heroes of the experiences we show and share, and which we probably hardly enjoy.

Or consider how our shopping habits have changed: we're learning to 'spend better', meaning that we 'google' a product before we make any decision about it. Before purchasing, we consult all possible reviews, comparative tests; we invest our time. In many areas, we trust influencers or other common users we deem as trustworthy because they are (or are perceived like) 'similar' to us.

Everything seems to be in our hands, but we pay a price. In data. People, companies, programs know our habits, our preferences, what we buy or like. Commercially speaking, what we can give to a company is stored in our computer cache memory, which also holds the choices we didn't make but wish we had (like a reservation for a holiday we only dreamt about) or the products we collected details about before buying them at a local street store.

This (somewhat 'dadaist') big data scenario is also changing the way we communicate as individuals, the way we interact with the information we're given and the way information is conveyed.

Today, digital technology allows us to communicate with anybody, anytime and at no cost. Digital era consumers can interact with the whole planet and contents are just a click away on their smartphones. Once, media were exclusively *one-way*; today, digital technology allows us to send messages or learn what's going on in the world in real time. While we read the news, get angry or comment something, Google logs everything, from our interactions to our car travels, and collects useful data.

An algorithm will then send us links to articles and tests confirming that 'X' is the best product around, and we'll believe we found out by ourselves. Our behaviors are logged. At all times. 24/7.

Companies need to understand that being on social media is not about advertising products, not anymore; they must develop a shared experience with their users and followers, and they need to carefully manage their customer relationships.

People are constantly distracted and hungry for contents, of any type. Generating genuinely interesting contents is one of the jobs of the future, as contents are going to be increasingly tailored around individuals.

That's why it's essential that businesses rely on storytelling: they need to tell stories that can spark emotions that are linked to their products' history and engage readers.

In storytelling, contents must be ceaselessly renewed, and brands must tell their audience and themselves stories with a silver thread that is increasingly focused on their products (for instance, a piece of clothing must be worn by a living person and placed within the context of a brand's identity).

The future of digital communication will increasingly rely on storytelling and on the extent a message is relevant to people. Relevancy comes from a message's ability to push users to perform an action: a 'Like', a share, a comment. These actions will then spread across the contacts of those who perform them.

People are media because communication is ensured by the people themselves, who reach out to other people, who in turn share their contents. It is important for a business to be aware that it's very easy for users to interact with companies today: all they need to do is send a Facebook message. This is an opportunity for improving consumer loyalty but it also exposes a company to errors and mistakes. That's why businesses really need a strategy that helps them understand their customers and communicate with them.

Some users will directly tell a company what's wrong with their products and services, but many others will simply leave a comment on Facebook, TripAdvisor, Booking, and this may be of some consequence for a company's reputation. In such cases, a business must promptly reply, but also log all interactions in order to grow and improve. That's why Customer Relationship Management (CRM) has extended to (big) data collection: to allow companies to make sure customers get a better service via tailored offers and, most of all, to predict the future of their mutual relationship. Artificial intelligence is only effective and capable of learning if it is fed with data. When it comes to the Internet of Things, which is becoming a bigger part of our lives, many actual concerns about privacy arise, but this is not may not be an issue for many people because of the services these 'things' grant them. Amazon's Echo is just the starting point of the interactive vocal storytelling of the future, a time when we'll interact 'with' (and not 'via') our devices, discarding tactile controls in favor of voice recognition. However, whatever revolution the human voice will bring, the *next big thing* will certainly be the Blockchain, a 'distributed ledger' that can trace transactions – in a non-hackable way, theoretically – and keep a log of people's digital signatures. This technology can be applied to any type of digital data, from bitcoins to medical records.

Since no central authority is needed as a guarantor, the involved parties can develop direct relationships. A Blockchain can also be applied to 'smart contracts', legally-binding agreements between private entities that are negotiated without the presence of notaries, lawyers or banks.

They ensure a greater freedom when it comes to settling terms but also prevent any fraud from either party, since Blockchain records cannot be tampered with.

Yes, this is the *next big thing*, and more will come.

To paraphrase historian Yuval Noah Harari, it's important that we try and put technology at the service of mankind, and not the other way around.

Introduction

This morning – still lying in my bed – I reached for my smartphone and just like every Mornico – still lying in my bed – I scrolled through my Facebook wall.

It's something we don't notice anymore and do on self-pilot. Estimatedly, we pick up our phones about 100 times a day (yes, one hundred: I bet you're now thinking you do it 4 or 5 times tops but no, it's actually one hundred) and spend almost one hour a day on Facebook (one hour on Facebook alone being much a longer time than our average lunch break).

So, this morning – still lying in my bed – I did five things on Facebook:

1) I 'Liked' a lovely sentence by a friend (whom I don't believe I've ever met in the flesh); it was nicely laid out against a preset blue backdrop with geometrical patterns. As a matter of fact, the sentence was not by my 'friend': it was the translation of a famed American comedian's line. Enter the first paradox of social networks: original contents count for only a fraction compared to 'Likes', retweets, quotations and shares in general. Social networks are an impoverished medium, where a user's actions are like a guitar's sounding board and people are the instrument. *People are media*, as we'll see. Enter the second paradox: the *echo chamber*. This is a phenomenon that, due to Mr. Zuckerberg's sophisticated algorithms, progressively fine-tunes Facebook's knowledge about us, our preferences and interests, our political orientation. It's meant to help us only get in touch with what we may be interested in. So, just like a good Mediterranean mother, a natural-born worrier, one of the world's five richest men is protecting me from myself, from bad news, from things I don't like, and fills my time (one hour a day, one 24th of my day - by extension, one 24th of my whole life) with food recipes, brief finance pieces, news about my favorite football team, upcoming album releases, art exhibitions.

Meanwhile, he's protecting other users from all of the above, while preventing me from seeing their fast cars, political views, hidden camera shows where people get hurt, luxury watches, tropical holidays, tattoos, cats, dogs and most of all the news about their favorite football teams.

2) With a reaction not dissimilar from suddenly witnessing some gruesomely devastated body in a car accident, I saw a picture of my ex's new partner.

They both look happy, all they do is smile and hug. He sports a beard, a side quiff and sunglasses. His face is like 1,000 other faces on my

Facebook wall. And another 100,000 I meet on the streets. They may be clones, they may be the same person.

Or it may be me, too old or too jealous. So I decided to block my ex. I can't stand seeing her so happy in places and situations she supposedly hated (or at least that's what she always told me). Whatever the reason, blocking her is the very last act of freedom I can exert.

3) I watched a time-lapse video about the making of gazpacho soup. It only takes ten seconds, at least on Facebook. I will cook it tonight, provided I don't find a different and more appealing video meanwhile.

4) I read a movie review, because a friend had commented a post about it. Actually, his wasn't a real comment, but a common friend's name he had 'tagged' by using the @ symbol. That's how you 'forward' contents on Facebook. ¾ of all comments are tagged names and surnames, and they mean: 'dear @namesurname, we were talking about/you may be interested in/you'll love *this*'. All without the hassle of writing an actual message.

5) Finally, I watched a video of a car accident captured by a security camera. I had to wait for a non-skippable 30-second ad break before I could 'enjoy' 8 seconds of a black and white portrait video. Very low quality material, with zero journalistic value. As a matter of fact, there was no journalistic content; it was some sort of 'low-level' production,

where 'low' was not its place in the hierarchy of content generation but a prior admission of its quality. Pretty low, indeed.

Finally, I managed to separate myself from my phone, drop it and get up from bed.

I went out and, while in the car, I listened to some radio. In order to pay a lower insurance fee I installed a device that ceaselessly transmits my cruising data along with my updated location. I had an affair with a co-worker once, and we went to a motel during our lunch break.

That motel's location is still inside my insurance company's database or whatever database the company might have sold to a third party ever since. Four years have passed and, while I've forgotten about it, my car hasn't.

Whenever I catch the underground, my annual subscription always 'knows' what stations I get on and off at.

A car sharing service 'sees' where I am, where I'm going, what time I'm back and knows if I stay too long at somebody's address after I have driven them home.

When I withdraw money from an ATM, the system knows the amount I'm getting and when I did the same operation in the past.

The same applies to the things I purchase with my credit card, how much I spend, what it means for my salary once it's added to my ATM withdrawals.

And last, I made some phone calls.

One, two, three calls. A system knows how long they lasted and whom I called. And most importantly, it knows where I've been, which cells I've locked onto, where I am right now, with a margin of error of just a couple of feet.

There are people, businesses, entities and programs that know where we are, what we buy, what we think and what we like.

They always know, even now, the very moment we're writing this and you're reading it.

Their knowledge about us evolves as they analyze our data.

They're inaccessible, invincible and very, very accurate. Digital technology is now an incontrovertible praxis for both consumers and companies.

The digital era consumer has created a parallel universe based on noble and less noble devices and on our ability to instantly communicate with the whole planet, to watch any content and carry a full library inside our smartphones, to check whether our home lights are on or out, to pick up and read our medical results from work or home.

On the other hand, companies are creating systems and algorithms to monitor and control their own performances and also consumers' lives.

These systems touch and overlap, because all involved parties need each other: companies sell and most of all acquire a growing amount of information so they can follow, trace and understand their customers; consumers get to read a book for free or compare a product price across hundreds of different providers and eventually find the best price, the best delivery option and, via user reviews, even a product's quality.

We'll analyze the digital era from its beginnings and try to understand how this evolution we cannot yet control is affecting our world; it destroys jobs, it takes the barriers of space and time down.

At the dawn of civilization we were quite quick to learn how to use fire to cook food, but the industrial revolution took a million years to happen.

Will it be the same for digital technology?

Hello. My name is Aldo, and Silvio.

I'm the latest Homo Sapiens release, the child of the digital age.

I wield my smartphone, I use it to take pictures of myself against a backdrop, *any* backdrop.

Chapter 1
THROUGH THE LOOKING GLASS

1.1 SELFIES: A REVOLUTION BROUGHT ABOUT BY REAR CAMERAS

1.2 EXPERIENCE: I AM YOUR MEDIA

1.3 REVIEW: THE TRUTH BEYOND FOCUS GROUPS

1.1 SELFIES: A REVOLUTION BROUGHT ABOUT BY *REAR* CAMERAS

You'll wander around Venice and won't notice it right away. And once you're in San Marco square, you won't even mind. You'll just do the usual tour and enjoy the cathedral, the 100-year-old bell tower apparently being there since forever, or the world's oldest café still in business, Caffè Florian, where an aperitif comes for the price of an iPhone. Then you'll walk towards the lagoon, keeping yourself on the square edge that faces the Canal Grande.

You'll stroll by Palazzo Ducale and keep left, headed to the Ponte dei Sospiri, the 'Bridge of Sighs'.

Made in Istrian limestone, this Baroque bridge has a chilling story that made it famous across the world. It passes over the Rio di Palazzo canal and connects the Doge's Palace to the Prigioni Nuove (New Prison) building.

Prisoners used to walk on this bridge when they were brought from their cells to the Inquisitor's interrogation room and be sentenced. Legend has it that at the times of the Most Serene Republic of Venice, they would deliver their last sigh as free men here: in the Doge's Republic, once you were sentenced you wouldn't come back.

Tourists come from every corner of the world to take pictures of this bridge. To properly do so, you need to be in one of the only two spots where you can actually see it: the Canonica bridge and the Ponte della Paglia (the one you access from San Marco square when you're headed to Riva degli Schiavoni). The latter is always crowded with people, because of its perfect line of vision onto the Bridge of Sighs, especially on summer evenings when it gifts you with one the most beautiful sunsets of Venice, the sun going down behind the Salute minor basilica. This is right where you realize that nobody halts you. Up until a couple of years ago, you could hardly walk on this bridge, not only for the huge mass of people posing for a photo but because most of them needed a 'photographer' to have their group pictures taken, and a random passer-by would be picked for the occasion. Since such 'photographers' needed to make a couple of steps back to fit everybody into the frame, for a handful of seconds nobody could actually walk in front of their cameras. Tourists would move in fits and starts and covering a bridge that is only a few meters long took some minutes.

It doesn't happen anymore. Tourists take selfies now.

This change may seem minimal, but it's actually epoch-making. The action itself has changed: people used to 'have their pictures taken', now they 'take their own pictures'. If you're not interested in capturing what's on your left or right, you can now cross the Ponte della Paglia in just a few seconds.

You may argue that self-timers have been featured on cameras all along. But the true revolution is seeing your own face *live*.

The true revolution is your smartphone's *rear* camera.

People's lives have changed. When they visit Venice, they take hundreds of pictures, as their phone and camera memories have become virtually limitless (younger generations will never experience the sheer terror of a film roll running out of shots). So, when they go back home and connect their phone to a computer, they end up with thousands of faces: their own.

This is the 'experience': a fixed subject (our own face) against a varying backdrop (a bridge, a bell tower, a gondola, a pigeon, whatever).

This is the *Zeitgeist*, the spirit of our times.

Why do people take selfies? Because a selfie is a flag you plant on the Moon.

Or the notch on the Red Baron's biplane, a tag's explication.

Once I used to take a picture and *then* comment: 'How beautiful Venice is'. Then I started tagging myself around Venice, and take pictures *later*. Very often it was a 'weird' picture, taken from an unusual angle or with a filter applied to it, enhancing or removing its colors so that it could get more 'Likes'. In the end I realized that the true reason why I take pictures of myself when I go to Venice is to post them on Facebook. So everything is reversed: my face is the main element now, while Venice, Rotterdam, the Machu Picchu or any other amazing or very-hard-to-reach place lies in the background. With my own face in the foreground. Mine, yours, ours.

If I were good looking, these pictures would be amazing.

Apparently, this phenomenon has a 'social' pursuit: as Francesco Bianconi, singer in the Italian band Baustelle, wrote in his song *A vita bassa*, it is an 'antidote to an anonymous future'.

Lack of self confidence obviously pervades our society and we all share it in varying degrees. Posting my selfie means I'll get some 'Likes' on Facebook or some (either positive and negative) comments from my friends on WhatsApp, and they'll all compensate for the concerns I have about myself.

Why do we take selfies?

And how do they impact our lives? Once we take for ascertained that something needs to become viral (a term from twenty years ago) to be successful in the 'digital world', we can legitimately ask ourselves what triggers such virality. And most of all, I wonder whether my face has the power to do it.

My 'beautiful' face is a testifying documentation of myself in the *here and now*, it says I'm a citizen of an 'exact tagged spot of the world', since such exact spot lies in the background. Here and now.

In his book *Human Race,*[1] Ian Mortimer introduces quite an interesting theory that traces the beginning of the Age of Enlightenment back to the invention of modern mirror manufacturing techniques, a fact that allowed us to build our self-awareness from our recognition of our own image and value.

In the 19th Century silver nitrates were discovered, allowing a significant lower cost than silver and gold, which were used for mirror-making during the Renaissance. A growing number of people could finally and clearly see their own faces for the first time. It may seem a little thing now but it was an amazing change, not unlike selfies (every age has the revolution it deserves, after all. *O tempora, o mores...*).

For the first time in human history, after people had ignored their own appearance, millions of faces were 'distributed'. It was a short step before 'self-awareness' was born.

---

[1] Ian Mortimer, *Human Race: Ten Centuries of Change on Earth.* Vintage, 2015.

1.2 EXPERIENCE: I AM YOUR MEDIA

In October 2013, a Soviet submarine suddenly emerged in the town centre of Milan, Italy. It was an advertising campaign, a publicity stunt conceived by M&C Saatchi for Genertel, an Italian insurance company. 'Anything can happen' was the claim. A hashtag was printed on the submarine turret.

The hashtag was there because, if a submarine peeks out of a concrete road a few steps from the Duomo cathedral, the first thing passers-by will do is take a picture they can share with their friends. The lowest common denominator of a submarine in downtown Milan is actually a picture.

The campaign proved to be extremely successful: over 80,000 people witnessed the real thing emerging from the pierced pavement. But the most striking fact was the over 100,000,000 Internet users who saw the 'Submarine in Milan' from pictures their contacts had posted on social networks.

Communication was hence ensured by the people, who reached out to other people, who in turn had probably shared the news to let other people know. So *people are media*, at all times: they are media for either

12 or 12,000 friends, or for 4 million users visiting the "Corriere della Sera" website to watch something fresh or unusual, mostly a picture or a video, published by a journalist who's found it on a friend's profile.

All great publishing groups are now on all major social networks. It's a matter of survival.

Google and Facebook are becoming 'the Internet', because they're the only websites that most of their online audiences visit.

According to a recent study by Pew Research Center, 44% of Americans look for news on Mark Zuckerberg's platform.[2] If they don't want to be outshined by Facebook's huge firepower, traditional media outlets need to launch social campaigns aiming at engaging their readers/users and encouraging the *journalist citizen* who lives inside each of us.

After a earthquake hit central Italy in August 2016, the social profiles of all major newspapers asked their followers to 'send their first pictures of the quake'.

It was a justified move: a professional photographer would have certainly taken some amazing and front page-worth pictures capturing the tragedy and destruction caused by Nature's blind fury, but a single photographer would've never been able to reach *all* the places hit by the earthquake. Also, everything on Facebook happens in real time,

---

[2] News Use Across Social Media Platforms 2016, May 2016
(http://www.journalism.org/2016/05/26/ news-use-across-social-media-platforms-2016/).

while a 'traditional' medium like a newspaper, with its old methods and routines, needs *at least* some time to find the proper pictures and people. Facebook makes everything quicker and easier.

How can a company (not necessarily in the publishing field) take advantage of this bulk of user-generated contents in an era when people develop a bond with some brands to the point of following them and sharing their values and social missions?

Once there were some 'super brands' people would grow an affection for. We all have met at least one 'Apple lover', somebody who takes up the cudgels for the latest Cupertino gadget. This experience is beginning to wane now: the affection for brands is becoming a nebula.

In the future, brands will have to become educators, or we'll all do it ourselves.

When I subscribed to Facebook, one of the first things I remember doing – right after snooping around the profiles of my former school friends to see what they had become – was to click the 'Like' button for brands such as Nutella or Coca-Cola. How couldn't I, after all? They're products I like very much. The funny thing, however, is that a second later I didn't know what do with those 'Likes'.

The real problem is when the brand itself doesn't know what to do with them.

1.3 REVIEW: THE TRUTH BEYOND FOCUS GROUPS

Every year, the Italian social study and research institute Censis issues a report about communication. Over time this report has become a reference point for newspapers, because of its ability to accurately portray Italy and Italians. It's seldom kind, but its judgments are based on actual figures. The 2016 report was titled *I media tra élite e popolo (Media, élites and common people)* and the title says it all. Tech insiders may keep on

TRADITIONAL MEDIA OUTLETS LAUNCH SOCIAL CAMPAIGNS AIMING AT ENCOURAGING THE 'JOURNALIST CITIZEN' WHO LIVES INSIDE OF US

praising new technologies and the Web, but television still pretty much rules the roost, with 97,5% of the population using it (that means *almost everybody*) with a 0.8% increase from 2015. TV is not dead at all: it's alive and kicking. Radio is quite healthy as well, with a 84.9% adoption rate. Paper press is the one that's actually suffering, with a 26.5% loss in readers over the last ten years. An utter disaster, since general readers are less than 40% of the Italian population. This figure pretty much applies to book readers, about 47%, with a 4.3% plunge from 2015. As for the Internet, it experiences a 2.8% increase in penetration in one year and reaches at 73.7%. A growth that is still distant from a full 100%, though.

Certainly online papers have grown in a similar way – +2% – but the goal is still to be reached. It's comforting to learn that 95.9% of people under 30 years of age say they're familiar with the Web: the much-celebrated *digital divide* keeps on shrinking.

'The tools of digital disintermediation are sneaking like wedges into the groove of imbalance that has been dug between the élites and the common people, serving the deconstruction of the different forms of legitimate authorities and flowing into the variable forms of an anti-systemic and radical populism that are rapidly spreading across Europe and the Western world'.

These words are from Censis, not your next-door blogger.

Also, the Italian institute confirms that social platforms are becoming increasingly pervasive: WhatsApp is the most widespread app (61.3%), followed by Facebook and YouTube. Let's not forget that WhatsApp can't be monitored and all conversations stay inside cell phones. By means of this daily increase in social platform users, who according to the 2016 Censis report amounted to 65% of the total population and feature a double-figure growth rate every year, we're migrating 'from a TV-centric to an ego-centric model'.

Censis goes even further and claims the Internet and new media are the main cause for the problems that modern Western democracies are currently facing, as social platforms push people towards 'forms of indifference' even among 'educated and politically/socially active subjects'. As journalist Luciano Capone noted on *Il Foglio*,[3] blaming new media for rebellions and juvenile impatience or indifference means choosing not to acknowledge most of our current social problems, from galloping unemployment rates to the inability of politics to respond to new challenges, and they have nothing to do with the Internet.

The Internet may be changing many things, but it's not that powerful.

The advent of digital technology has transformed our perception of time and space. It has happened very quickly and many breakthroughs are so revolutionary that sometimes we wonder how we could live without them.

Just think of the last time you wrote a letter and sent it via your traditional mail service. The invention of email was a breaking point under many aspects: it allowed us to save time and money and to be

---

[3] Luciano Capone, *Indifferenza, populismo e crisi delle élite. È tutta colpa di internet!*, in Il Foglio, 29th September 2016 (http://www.ilfoglio.it/dati-e-statistiche/2016/09/29/news/indifferenza-populismo-e- crisi-delle-elite-e-tutta-colpa-di-internet-104669)

always accessible even when we're not at home. Those of us who write, the former teenagers from the Eighties, belong to the last generation who can still recall experiencing a time *before* and a time *after*. We had so much more freedom *before*.

Today, we take it for granted that we're always traceable and people can reach us in just a few seconds, anytime. In the past, when we had to meet someone, we would agree on a place and a time.

IN ITALY, A MARKET RESEARCH IS VERY HARD TO PERFORM: ITALIANS ARE INSINCERE BY NATURE AND CHARACTER

If the other party was there waiting for us, everything was fine, mission was accomplished. If we were the first to arrive, we knew we had to wait and we did, uncomplainingly. If half an hour later the wait proved to be vain, we could safely go home: the agreed rule was that we didn't have long-term obligations.

When we were young, we'd go out and tell our mother: 'See you at 8'. Until we came back, varyingly on time, our parents had no way to know where we were and if we would be late for dinner. Now, we all use WhatsApp.

When we'd go out, all that was on our minds was meeting with our friends. We'd agree on getting together at an exact place and time. But how many times someone wouldn't show up?

About twenty-five years ago my university friends and I were in Rome and decided to go out. We were about sixty people, we were supposed to meet in piazza Venezia, under the balcony Mussolini gave his speeches from. We waited for 1.5 hours to allow everybody to get there; mobile phones were not yet common – for how absurd it may seem today – and we would find a way to kill time. Today, someone would immediately text 'Where are you?', a anxiety generator that may even improve the punctuality of Italians. On the other hand, when we're the ones who are late, the very first (and quite predictable) thing we do is to shamelessly lie. And if our excuses are not credible enough, new technologies come to our rescue: every last generation smartphone provides specific functions that allow us to learn and potentially share our exact location and the time needed to get to a meeting point. A lie we tell gets easily geo-localized and all we can do is admit the truth: we dozed off or got distracted.

Social networks have helped us develop an in-depth knowledge of our superficial relations (let's admit it: there are at least 100 people on Facebook you know everything about but you haven't met in person for a long time!) and we pay some frantic attention to people's behaviors.

In trying to make some interesting characters out of ourselves, we've told a lot about ourselves and we still ceaselessly do, in real time, to the point of giving away our freedom and, most of all, our right to lie.

Italy is a country where a market research is very hard to perform, as Italians are intrinsically insincere, by nature and character. And about everything. Just think about politics: when elections are held and exit polls are performed outside of ballot boxes, results usually deviate from the actual election results. This happens on a regular basis, not occasionally.

We're also insincere when it comes to love. Whether it's an actual feeling for another individual, or our 'love' for a product or a brand. If you ask Americans when and how much fat food they eat during the day, they have no problem telling you the truth: 'I'll have a double cheeseburger at lunch, and a large-size Coke at dinner...'.

Ask an Italian if he eats French fries and he'll reply: 'No way, it happens twice a month, tops'.

And while he tells you so, he'll have his fingers dirty with salt and his cupboard is jam-packed with snacks.

Back in the Forties, American sociologist Robert King Merton became famous for establishing an innovative research methodology for human and social sciences, the much celebrated 'focus group'. His starting point was an apparently simple concept, which had already been used to analyze the effects of political propaganda: you pick up a group of people and invite them to discuss a topic. We usually deal with marketing focus groups, where people discuss an advert, an idea, a product, but any topic can actually be covered.

Participants are asked some questions by a supervisor, usually the researcher himself. They can talk to other guests, exchange opinions, refute their thoughts. In theory, such discussions provide an interesting feedback via critiques, suggestions and concerns and they help identifying the best audience for a product before it lands on supermarket shelves. Hopefully, this is a way to understand how to make a success out of an item once it is marketed.

Today, we can safely say that focus groups are of no use. You'll always have the same scenario: some sort of prefixed dynamics with one individual taking the floor and never leaving it. Basically, the group members rely on a 'know-all' who feels the urge to express his opinion, something about which the other participants could not care less once they'll leave the room. They simply agree with a (self-) appointed leader because within that closed environment they can work less harder and waste as little time as possible.

The amazing fact is that all focus groups end up with an unanimous result. Discussions and confrontations are not encouraged, but deemed as useless. Everybody simply says 'Yes, I agree with him/her' and maybe throw in a couple of adjectives. Just like when we were not ready for a test at school.

Participants just stuff themselves with crisps and then go home with a 20€ fuel voucher after wasting an evening they'll never get back (at one point the focus group business had to be regulated, as it had become a job for some people: prizes included fuel vouchers, jackets, food, almost anything).

Today, companies can't rely on analog and obsolete techniques, they need to take advantage of an all-round technology.

Collecting data is essential but not enough: you also need to be able to read, analyze and interpret them.

The solution are *enriched data*.

People really *are* media. On Twitter, everybody tweets whatever goes through their minds. In the majority of cases, they do it to show off, to feel cool or to protest against something. These are primary feelings and, if we skim off all the fake accounts, they express real emotions.

By simply applying some semantics to a platform like Twitter, we could really sample the country in real time.

Businesses can follow the changing mood of their audience and learn in real time if they're in a positive or negative phase.

Given the huge amount of available information, we could learn what Italians or specific target groups (i.e., 24-year-old girls who live in Northeast Italy and have spent the last 12 months abroad after high school) think of a given brand.

However, it's true that, either on social networks and in focus groups (or on the street), you always get the outcome you're looking for if you ask the right question in the most appropriate way and with a proper blend of NLP and old-time craftiness.

In the Seventies a famous Italian TV commercial used to ask to casual consumers: 'Would you swap two boxes of washing powder with the one you're about to buy?' Respondents would decline but the only possible and reasonable answer should have been: 'No, of course I want two'.

However, if you manage to arrange your question in the most convincing way, people will go for just one box, the one you're advertising. The key to our credibility as communicators lies here and it dates back to the Sixties, when we started to make people believe in things that couldn't be. We would create amazing situations that got them estranged from the real world: talking hippos, *carmencita* dolls, magicians, talking chameleons, good looking 25-year-old mothers filling their teenager children with attentions and snacks. A gigantic fraud based on parallel worlds that couldn't last forever.

Instead, the new communication paradigm is based on *truth* and *reality*, and actually starts from the people. When they're online, people tell the truth. As false as Italians may be, this applies to them as well. We just need to tune in to them.

So let's deploy the proper tools, let's start to use them like they do abroad, especially in the USA.

When we post a sarcastic or ironic comment on a social network, our readers can tell if it is positive or negative.

Emotions are the foundation of a new consumer-business relationship.

US companies believe that the moment they lose a customer is the best to ask them a crucial question about their brand.

A customer's behavior necessarily influences a company' behavior and can ultimately help improving the world. The main goal for businesses is to act so they can better serve their customers. If they could understand what people want, and when and how, brands would never launch wrong or bad products anymore. Imagine you wanted to open a restaurant and you could read people's opinion on the Internet (a place where such info are easily found): you'd realize what is the most sough-after restaurant typology, along with its preferred location, and you would act with a very limited risk.

This kind of asset, though, has some specific features that differentiate it from others: a mortgage, say, is not a wearable device, the latter having a much higher purchase frequency. A mortgage may be taken out only once in a lifetime or at very distant time intervals. However, the analysis of one single purchaser allows us to extract a set of extremely useful socio-demographic information: their spending power, their online behavior, their geographical location, the kind of car they own.

Our goal is to learn if this socio-demographic profile is confirmed in reality and has a tendency to repeat over time. Market researches are performed over a wide population sample, and if we can steadily pinpoint a profile that has taken out a mortgage in the last few months we could then project such trend onto a number of *lookalike* profiles. We would learn which profiles within our target will possibly buy a house and we could lay out an online strategy to communicate our business proposal to them. Here is an actual and tangible example: you already know that individuals who are looking for a mortgage are 33% more likely to subscribe to a pay TV channel. Once you have acquired this data based on your agreements with third parties, you'll try and capture these people's profiles to feed them your advertisements: you'll submit your pay TV ads to all *lookalike* profiles who are potential mortgage takers. You'll obtain a blend of your analysis of your existing customers and their potential behaviors, and you'll use it to serve your message in the most targeted way and deliver the most suitable ad to the most suitable audience.

To do so you need to own the data, classify them in the best possible way and then act. Anybody can get the data, but not everybody can process and organize them and turn them into efficient assets for their business. Data about all different mortgage offerings have always been available, but no bank has ever thought about setting up an online service such as Mutuionline.it, which guides users who seek the best available mortgage. All the while, collecting their data.

Chapter 2

THE DIGITAL CITIZEN

2.1 THE '**SOCIAL**' **SOCIETY**

2.2 OUR LIFE IS STORED IN THE **CACHE MEMORY** OF OUR COMPUTER

2.3 CHATTING AS A PRIMARY **COMMUNICATION NEED**

2.4 IN LOVE WITH AN **ARTIFICIAL INTELLIGENCE**

2.5 HOW **MAJORS ARE DICTATING** THE NEW **RULES** FOR **ADVERTISING**

2.6 BLOCKCHAIN, THE **'NEXT BIG THING'** THAT WILL CHANGE THE MARKETING WORLD

2.7 INDUSTRY 4.0 AND RULING BY PLATFORMS

2.8 THE NEW STATE: **HYPER-CONTROL** VS. **HYPER-PARTICIPATION**

2.1 THE 'SOCIAL' SOCIETY

Social media have some great potential but lack dignity, and they have a very bad reputation. Many people deem them as shallow tools, nice for sharing jokes and reconnecting with lost friends, but I strongly believe we should reconsider: social media need be thoroughly studied so we can learn their limitations and use their countless abilities. Let's start from the cons, which coincidentally are over-amplified by other media, especially newspapers: social media are the 'cause' for cyber-bully and for our dissociation from reality. These disapprovals are nothing new, and probably just an exaggerated phenomenon of our times. When I was a kid, there was a bullied child in every school I went to. He would suffer bad pranks, threats, and violence. Still today, decades later, I can clearly remember his pain. Internet hadn't even been invented back then, and horrible things would be regularly inflicted in school corridors or yards. I'm pretty sure that, since the invention of school itself, you could find a student being picked on in every classroom around the world.

Every now and then, some old pictures from the Fifties resurface online: you'll see a group of people on a coach, a bus or a tram, all of them reading their newspapers, none of them looking out the windows or talking to another passenger. I'm inclined to think these were educated men and women: I can hardly picture a farmer of the time travelling by bus and, even if so, he wouldn't wear those clothes, let alone read a newspaper. Yesterday, I was travelling by the M1 underground train in Milan and had a quick look around: all passengers had their smartphones in their hands, their heads down to their device. All social classes were there: a manager, a housewife, an immigrant in his saggy clothes. I could only tell their social differences from their screens: the manager was flipping through the news, the housewife was chatting via WhatsApp, a young man was scrolling his social network profile, a woman from the Philippines was playing an extremely loud version of *Candy Crush*. And then, magically, everything changed and the manager, now on *Candy Crush*, had suddenly smashed the Filipino woman's score! These examples help me debunk a myth: except for a very few cases, social networks aren't directly responsible for cyber-bully or dissociation from reality (and negative phenomena in general). Users were already cyber-bullied on Irc chats, a true milestone for nostalgic geeks like myself. What I'm prone to admit is that the growth of communication media and the way they can be easily used and 'owned' has highly increased the magnitude of bad behaviors. It was much harder to badmouth somebody on TV or on the radio in the Nineties, and when it happened it was a striking fact. The resulting shame even drove some people to commit suicide.

Digital technology is, among many other things, a chance we must take. It's not about the medium, though: it's about us. We must learn to use the tools we have. We must master their potential and risks. For that matter it's adults, not young people, who mainly suffer the pervasiveness of media. Today, a smartphone is not different from what a TV set was in the Seventies. My mother's telly is on all day. She won't watch it, just listen to it. The noise coming from her television is an uninterrupted background. Famous voices talking to her pointlessly, ad breaks, music jingles, sound effects: they all try to catch her attention, in vain. She's often in some other room, doing something else. She'd probably feel much better without all that noise.

But she'd never turn off her TV, and she won't, Auditel[4] notwithstanding (which considers millions of mothers like mine as real, alive and participating viewers, whom advertising sales agencies sell for big bucks to companies that only invest to add their noise to this worthless ambient soundtrack). The most interesting factor here is actually my mother's (apparent) disaffection with television. The truth

---

[4] 'Auditel is a totally independent and impartial company that measures television audiences in Italy on a national and regional level through the various broadcasting modes.' (Source: www.auditel.it)

is that this clamoring, passive and intrusive medium has somehow inoculated itself into her and her decision-making processes.

'That's what the TV said', I often hear her say like a mantra, 'TV' being a synonym for absolute truth. Today, the same applies to a number of my peers when it comes to Facebook and the rest of new media. They just can't say no to them, I see them at restaurants, as they scroll their timelines or check their WhatsApp messages. More than anything, they believe in every hoax they read. It's a true addiction: adults on social media totally lack the ability to filter out fake contents, an ability that the younger generations will hopefully develop.

So the problem is not the medium, but what it conveys. The problem is culture, meaning our attitude towards things. Digital technology is like a remote control, perfect for switching channels. An inattentive, shallow observer may believe the digital world is a huge display of nothingness, of acute ignorance just being shown off. **In reality, digital technology is an evolution, not an involution.**

That's why a 'culture of culture' is essential; without it, users wouldn't – or shouldn't – be able to use digital tools.

The problem lies in measure – which rhymes with culture. As Italian writer, journalist and satirist Michele Serra puts it: the Web contains something so imponderable that makes it a qualitatively different medium from those that came before it.

Culture is not about owning or reading books: it's about mastering the tools we need to be the owners of our own thoughts. Smartphones make us believe we'll never get bored and always have something to do, read or watch. Social apps are just like heaven when it comes to spending our time. And if there's nothing new on Facebook, I can just swap to Instagram and look at a friend's or celebrity's picture. Then I can write to a couple of people on WhatsApp, expecting them to reply right away. Last, I'll read some news online.

Hours will go by, and I'll do all of these things very quickly, as the rules of this game demand. I'll never stop to really enjoy the pictures, I'll be annoyed if my

A 'CULTURE OF CULTURE' IS ESSENTIAL: WITHOUT IT, USERS WOULDN'T BE ABLE TO USE DIGITAL TOOLS

messages don't get an immediate reply. I'm always in a hurry and I don't even know why. **The keyword for Citizen 3.0 is 'entertainment'.**

The quickness of social platforms and new media has turned every indignation, protest, piece of news into a transient thing, and this applies to the cartoon jokes I post on my profile or the 'good morning' memes my aunt sends me every morning. Equally bound to rapidly disappear are the scandals of an old man being abused in a nursing home, of a girl being raped, of a migrant drowning. It happened to Aylan's body, the child who dreamt of a better future away from the Syria war, but died in the sea between Turkey and Greece. We were all shocked and posted our images, our tear-jerking phrases, our Gandhi aphorisms, our digital shouts against our insensitive politicians.

In two or three days something else will get our attention.

Sometimes an afternoon is just enough for Facebook to be filled up with something else, maybe an unjustified football penalty kick. Not unlike channel surfing in search for something I like on TV, I use my smartphone as a digital remote control to find a website with my next diversion.

A mobile phone is so easy and effortless to use.

Apps – a brilliant idea that was already featured on the very first iPhone – simplify my life to the point that I don't need to do anything. When I used my mobile phone like a computer, I had to go through all the hassles of desktop surfing: the URL typing, the hard-to-read tiny screen, the many buttons to click.

Now apps do everything, and they only give me one option to interact with. They want my data in return, but they allow me to save time.

Time, time, time: an asset that is running low, or at least this is what we want to believe. That's why we all want more of it.

Young people are even more fascinated by digital entertainment than adults. A journalist once told me how shocked he was when he found out that, when they discuss politics on Facebook, young people tend to laugh at fake and true news indifferently.

That's how it works, after all: they use these tools more ironically than adults, who tend to partake in things with sometimes unrestrained anger and/or passion.

On the other hand, young kids and children tend to prefer YouTubers and influencers who are seldom politically or socially active – those who are only play by social media rules, getting angry at something different every day – and make videos about make-up techniques, gaming and the very ordinary things they do. It's probably an age thing, just like when my father would only watch the newscast on TV while I loved music shows. Or maybe it's just a matter of how good young people are at taking media less seriously.

We all watch TV together, but apart. When *MasterChef* is on TV, we share our opinions on WhatsApp about what participant we'd like to kick out, or post witty lines on Twitter to get a retweet or a compliment. We have introduced the concept of *second screen*, which may suggest that we have an omnipresent small interactive screen in our hands to communicate with our friends while we watch TV. But it's not like that. Our device screen is our *first* screen. Our TV is on only as a driver for our online interactions. As a matter of fact, TV is our *second screen*.

I feel like I'm surrounded by care and affection because somebody is thinking about me. The truth is there's nobody with me on the couch, except maybe a dog lying on the floor and fantasizing about what's outside the closed window.

When I'm on a social medium, I close myself off without feeling lonely. This is a brand new phenomenon.

When I write a letter, I know that nobody is right in front of me and when I'm talking on the phone there's always a voice to keep me company. Today I always have a screen. Nobody is ever alone online. Or better: on social media.

Just try and write to somebody on WhatsApp: they will reply, even if they don't want to, because they feel they ought to or they fear that, if they don't, they may be left out from future chats. Just open your Online Friends list and you'll find someone to say 'Hi' to. We're talking about real friends here, people we know or have shared a moment with in real life and added as a contact or included in our phone's Address Book. **But there's another world of acquaintances out there called**

'groups' and its huge potential was totally grasped by Mark Zuckerberg. Facebook groups are the best place to go when you feel alone, as you'll always find somebody who reacts to some provocation, provided it's in line with the group's topic. Groups are a Citizen 3.0's cafés, a place where you can find somebody willing to chat even on New Year's Eve.

Groups are the practical adaptation of Seth Godin's digital tribes, only 100 times more powerful than forums. This is only because Facebook is always at hand. While I tend to 'Like' pages in a random fashion, I only subscribe to groups which I'm really interested in, otherwise I'd be flooded with spam.

A group is made of people who feel and think like me, so I focus on and identify with them; they become the place where I like to talk, where I look for updates, where my opinions are influenced. A group becomes my own sect.

The leader I reach out to is my group's moderator, whom I invoke for getting rid of 'trolls', who I do not necessarily see as fake accounts trying to break my group's equilibrium, but as people who question our shared truth. As Mark Schafer and Scott Crichlow suggest, groups where bonds are very tight tend to develop their own morality, and members seek unanimity, accept self censorships and most importantly deem people from outside the group as *enemies*. Together everything is possible, being together can only spawn beliefs. The very concept of society is overturned.

According to the 2017 European SPES Institute report, the number of vegans in Italy has tripled in just one year, and this is also due to an increase in social media communication by those who adhere to this philosophy of life. I say this with no judgment. These people look for a social confirmation, they need to extend their community. **The more people think like us, the more we're convinced our opinions are correct.** What we usually overlook is that we love being esteemed by our counterparts. That's why we try to be as 'appropriate' as we can get, by saying something that will certainly be appreciated.

Not only general thinking is never questioned, but news that reinforce it are only posted. Little by little, this attitude also shapes the way those who write the news think, and they end up adapting themselves in order to be accepted.

A vegan who lives in the Mugello area, a land of hunters and boar meat gravy, is still a vegan who thinks as a vegan.

The company he works for is not different from the companies where hunters work, as it is his income, and his house. Any market research based on demography would put the vegan in the same *cluster* as these hunters, with the same voting and purchase orientations. The reality is just the opposite, though: vegans may live a hundred miles away from each other, but the Web allows them to share information and make choices that are influenced by the thinking of the group they feel they belong to.

A vegan will never vote for a pro-hunting politician nor buy a pair of leather shoes. It's a true revolution. In the past, choices were influenced by conversations at cafés, now everything happens on Facebook.

When I clam up and stay inside my 'group' – intended as a reality I identify with – I tend to have the same bad behavior as the group, and I don't even realize.

Here's an example: some time ago, a lady from Massignano, a small town in Central Italy, apologized with the President of the Italian Chamber of Deputies, Laura Boldrini, after grossly slamming her on a social network. Her reply to the La Repubblica journalist asking about her motives really hit me: 'I don't even know why I did it, it must have been the anger I feel when I'm back from work. I'm 61, I was denied a disability pension despite having undergone three back surgeries. They say my pain is not work-related, but the truth is I broke my vertebrae when manufacturing shoe uppers and working in a restaurant's kitchen. I also need to help my family on the fields, or they won't survive. I didn't mean to offend the President, my insult was pretty much against everybody. I was tired, after a long day of work, and I must have read something that sounded like injustice to me, but I'm not holding it against her, how am I supposed to use my judgment? I tell you, I was ignorant'.[5] So, apparently, she wasn't really angry with President Boldrini but, since many people were, she followed in their footsteps and let off her anger against her.

All of this used to happen in the past as well, when people would gather up, organize protests that would become violent, with people being battered or even killed. Two differences remain, though: first, in the past you needed to actually leave your house and meet with people, and you would grow such a strong sense of belonging that a physical clash may occur. Apparently, this happens much less today, to the point that there's a brand new Italian word for these individuals: 'leoni da tastiera', 'keyboard lions' who are excellent at 'roaring' behind a computer screen but hide when they step outside their homes. On the other hand, it's once again a matter of time: **everything is quick, offences are quick, anger must be quick to build up and quick to wane so we can concentrate on some other stuff we can complain about.**

---

[5]http://www.repubblica.it/cronaca/2016/11/27/news/il_personaggio_le_sue_offese_sui_social_res e_note_dalla_presidente_della_camera_e_ora_maria_si_scusa-152908833/

Quickness and a limited attention span not only apply to negative passions, though: street or topic committees abound, with frequent but short-lived meetings, while political rallies held by traditional parties are increasingly deserted. On Facebook social topics are always on the agenda. Pages are filled with pictures of hearts being posted for sick children, but charity associations only find people for one-off events or short periods of time, or meet a higher number of benefactors but with a less continuative engagement. We all must get used to this level of inconsistency. The Web imposed it upon us.

2.2 OUR LIFE IS STORED **IN THE CACHE MEMORY OF OUR COMPUTER**

Does the average Italian know that anybody (including the government or a private business) could take a snapshot of their computer contents and learn their online behavior, their interests and preferences, the amount of pictures of cats, tattoos and exotic beaches they have viewed?

A company can learn all of this and accurately read into it to its own benefit.

The brands that are closer to the people are those that ceaselessly listen to users' behaviors and change their products and customer experience accordingly, in real time.

You'll find the following motto in every United States Postal Service office: 'Neither snow nor rain nor heat nor gloom of night stays these couriers from the swift completion of their appointed rounds'. A wonderful concept that tells us a lot about the USA. Nowhere else in the world people identify as much with their jobs. Every job is worthy of a person and every person is worthy of their job.

In America, a postman (just like a street sweeper, a salesperson, a laborer or anybody else) knows that he's working for everybody else, for the collectivity and himself.

People do their jobs as best as they can, with dignity and a sense of belonging. And they all, from the

THE REAL LIFE OF USERS IS STORED IN THE CACHE MEMORY OF THEIR COMPUTER

humblest operator to the most accomplished manager, receivea fair acknowledgment

THE TRUE LIFE OF EACH OF US LIES IN THE CACHE MEMORY OF OUR COMPUTERS

of their work from the collectivity. Our real, true and non-retouched life isn't the one we show on our Facebook wall or Twitter timeline. It's not even in the secrets we confide to our closest friends or to our partners. The true life of each of us, at least the one that is commercially appealing, is stored in the cache memory of our computers.

All the things we can say (and give) to brands are there. **The truth about ourselves is stored in our browser memories.** We can lie to anybody except Google. Every summer we look up 'Polynesia' but we spend our holidays on an Adriatic Sea beach with our family. If there's a huge difference between words and deeds, words are now on a digital medium, and the truth is a piece of big data, stored somewhere.

My cache memory knows if I wish I had gone to Samoa instead of Cesenatico. Can banks learn that I need a loan, then? It would be so useful for them, because buying credit is a complex process that take place once or twice in a lifetime (except for some irredeemable cases which are a sign of the times as well). How can banks 'listen' to us online to the point they can anticipate a need?

All the things we won't have done, all the things we'll have carefully reviewed will be in our cache memory, not even in our brain memory. Our irrational, true, hot life and our native consumerism are all there. We just need to learn how to extract them.

Furthermore, you can't take it for granted that customers will buy a loan online, regardless of how relevant it is to them in a given moment. They may obtain it after calling or visiting a bank branch; also, it's quite a widespread routine to consult products online and then finalize purchases at a point of sale. But what if a bank owns the right technology to easily identify target users who are looking for a loan and then send them a number of ad hoc email messages that increase their likelihood of contacting the bank and get that offer?

All businesses, regardless of technologies, have a route to follow. Different (potential) behaviors correspond to two different user types: those who are close to completing their purchase and promptly act because they've already made a decision and those who might be interested in purchasing (but there's no guarantee about it). When I want a new car or smartphone and I'm in the final stage of my decision, that's when I go to Google or a specific website and finalize my purchase. If I do so it's because my behaviors and data include me in the specific customer category that is close to what a business wants to sell me.

Conversations, especially those on Twitter, can be fully and usefully analyzed: on social media people tend to appear nicer and smarter than what they are, but also more discriminating.

Facebook introduced the 'thumb up' concept but most of Facebook posts and comments have a negative quality. That's exactly what happens with customer services: when a company, even the most virtuous, posts something, it is flooded with complaints.

A brand's page is pure customer service. It's not institutional anymore, and that's because whatever a business does becomes a communication channel. This tendency to comment is increasingly negative or conveyed towards indifference. Companies should never open a social channel, a toll free number or a support centre if they're not ready to receive complaints or – even worse – if they can't or don't want to manage it. If my original iPhone freezes, I simply reset it and smile. If a Chinese clone phone freezes I throw it in the garbage can, because it is not a *lovemark*, a brand I'm madly in love with (more on *lovemarks* later). Maybe it's time we start to show our shortcomings, and bring out the *underdogs*, the things that survive because of their faults. Just like Pippo Franco[6], who's always been perceived as funny and fascinating despite his gigantic nose. Every brand has its own strengths and weaknesses, so what must their future on social media rely on? Should they be ready to expose themselves to negative comments or use their social channels with no interactions at all?

In cinema, the idea of 'truth' – starting from Edgar Morin – has been covered a lot. In 1997's *Liar Liar*, Jim Carey stars as Fletcher Reede, a successful lawyer who tells lies over lies to make sure his clients win their lawsuits. In his private life, however, his approach proves to be faulty and prevents him from having a relationship with those who are close to him. When his son Max's dream of having a non-lying father comes true, Reede finds himself in deep trouble, as he can't lie anymore, not only in complex or work circumstances, but also when he faces small everyday deeds. In his 2009 movie *The Invention Of Lying*, director and actor Ricky Gervais pictures himself in a world where nobody tells lies, until he realizes he can lie for his own personal gain. These Hollywood and dystopian situations, strikingly similar to the *Black Mirror* TV series, come to mind when you consider the

---

[6] An Italian actor, comedian, television presenter, and singer.

'experiment' performed, this time in real life, by Antoine Garrot in 2013. A 26-year-old French male nurse from Rennes in France, Garrot woke up one morning and, tired of lies, hypocrisies and fabrications, decided to stop lying, at least on Facebook. So, to a friend who had posted her picture in search for some (self-righteous, according to Antoine) compliments from her friends, he quietly replied that, had he been her, he wouldn't have gone looking for compliments on Facebook. Similarly, Antoine told a contact who had posted his usual show-off about his Corsica holidays ('A quick Mojito on our hotel's terrace! Tomorrow morning we'll go fishing. I do love Corsica! Isn't life beautiful!??') that he had always been unhappy and should restrain himself from fabricating lies.

Garrot's experiment lasted 24 hours: after just one day of sheer 'truth' his Facebook friends had halved. Antoine didn't dishearten, as he admitted he only knew half of the people who had left. This story shows the two sides of the coin: one is our will to show off and tell a version of ourselves that is close to what we wish we were like, rather than what we really are. The other is we give some (false) gratification to people by appreciating them for what they wish they were and not for what they really are. And then there's friendship, a term we should always question, since on social platforms we call 'friends' people we have never met. And yet, when we're online, we lightheartedly give away details about ourselves that we would never share. We do so because we're sure we won't be criticized on Facebook. This may explain why so many people are so embarrassed when they're bashed online; it's something they don't expect to happen in an place that is normally filled with smiles and compliments.

Bianco Martinot, a sociologist and professor at the Faculty of Sociology in Rennes underlines: 'Most of the people who felt they were victims of Antoine's comments know he is right but, socially and most of all in public, this is considered an act of war'. Nevertheless, he deemed the shock effect of the young French's comments as 'necessary': 'There are people who refuse to accept the truth and don't want to acknowledge some aspects of their lives, such as their partner's mediocrity or their physical appearance. Here is where Antoine hits hard, to a shocking effect: it's never pleasant but, at least in my opinion, needed.'

Probably, Antoine's experiment is not successful because the world likes a happy ending. We all lash out against anything when we're online, but it's something we're not supposed to ride on.

We haven't yet covered some behaviors that are related to how technologies, and our affection towards some topics (ethics and the environment above all), can change our lifestyle and behaviors. I'm talking about our huge (facilitated and not negative) use of *wearable devices*, our brand new form of consumerism, the digital items that allow us to share our activities. Like our running session at the park. Recently, people have been going crazy for a hydrogen-making kit you can install in your car. Those who sell the kit claim it ensures 20-50% savings on fuel. You can purchase it from a social network profile, find the instructions online and even install it yourself, if you're good at it. This marks an acceleration in trends and interests and in behaviors that would've been rejected not so long ago. A man from Teramo, Italy, is currently requesting the FCA homologation for a car running on oxyhydrogen. It requires a small computer that impacts fuel and early tests seem to confirm quasi-zero emissions. It practically turns gasoline into water. With cars actually running fast.

The greatness of digital technology, the beauty of a man who builds, writes and invents things lies here as well. What a single individual can do is striking and many things can be changed by starting from the bottom and sharing knowledge. Just like the ability to light up a house with no electricity, using a water bottle: this may mean so much for places like the suburbs of a huge Asian and African city or a village in Amazonia. It's a 2-watt appliance: almost nothing, technically speaking, but it represents the absolute difference between darkness and light.

Internet has put a spotlight onto this invention, spread it around and made it an actual solution for many poor places around the world. Once upon a time, when TV was still relevant, only two 'TV-ready' scientists were regularly invited to Italian shows: Carlo Rubbia and Antonino Zichichi. They were the only ones who could be shown on television because they had turned science into a fascinating story: 'Atoms and molecules were within everyone's reach and a single atom could be a sweater, as red as a steak', I still remember this line. Today, TED allows scientists that once were unsuitable for TV to make their 20-minute speech and have their own audience.

In Italy, a Japanese girl named Akiko Makiko has made a TED-like platform that gives our talents some exposure. She made a live streaming on a news website once, an iTalk featuring a number of Italian country managers, Uber's Italian country manager and so on. I really thought nobody could be interested, but 110,000 people watched it. With no need to mention or show some beautiful girl's body!

Companies just don't understand: they're economically capsizing because of digital technology. Think about the MelaScrivi platform: a user logs in, posts a brief and people write an article from it. And how does the business react to it? By buying the platform. The risk, though, is that the next intuition will surpass the current one. The only action that companies can take at this stage is to surrender to their acquisition 'bulimia': they become bigger and bigger so they can interact with masses and be able to react to digital innovations and social changes. **If you don't innovate you die; if you innovate too quickly, you die as well.** Ever wonder why there only three major beer companies in Italy? Because craft beer is growing locally. If supermarkets sell a major beer brand for 1.20 Euros a bottle and only earn 0.5 Euros a bottle, they need to have a big logistics model in place that allows them to buy thousands of beer bottles and, because of current aggressive bundle polices, the beer manufacturer's other products as well. Beer crafters produce much smaller quantities, but sell a bottle for 7 Euros with a 6 Euro net gain while also building a reputation for quality that allows them to win premium customers. Big companies will then try and survive by buying out other medium-to-big brands, because they need to have huge volumes out on the market, but waste a lot of glass in the process and eventually resort to trying to buy out the small craft beer brands. If you think about it, the success of craft beers is a result of digital technology. Craft beer manufacturers can exchange recipes and methods, they can communicate quickly and most of all they can look trendy and cool on social media. Hipsters, so analogical in their ways but so inherently digital, will come in hordes.

2.3 CHATTING AS A PRIMARY COMMUNICATION NEED

Communication is among a human's primary needs. Since the dawn of time, beside eating, sleeping and reproducing, we have always looked for a way to express our thoughts, feelings and fears.

The rise of digital has been *disruptive* for this as well. Today, anybody can communicate to anyone, whenever they want, at no cost and instantly. Social networks give a potentially unlimited audience to each one of us.

However, one tool we all use every day has become essential for communication, much more than social networks: a chat.

On a typical day of an average human being, the most used communication tool is undoubtedly a chat. The overriding majority of the planet's inhabitants use WhatsApp, Telegram, Facebook Messenger, WeChat, iMessage and other similar services on a daily basis.

According to the 'Digital In' 2017 research by *We Are Social*, WhatsApp and Facebook Messenger users exceed 1 billion units each, there are more than 800 million people on QQ and WeChat, 300 million Snapchat users, and so on.

These tools are free, user-friendly and easy-to-use. If you try and imagine the amount of messages that are exchanged everyday around the world, it's easy to get dizzy.

For some time now, all major instant messaging services have provided voice messages: we're back to using our voices again, not to make phone calls (they're freefalling, as are SMS messages), but to communicate 'to' a device that acts as a channel for our voice messages to the person we're contacting.

We don't talk to a friend anymore: we entrust a phone with doing it on our behalf.

What may seem the latest technology breakthrough is actually the beginning of a new era.

Psychologist Dan McAdams has introduced the concept of 'narrative identity', a theory that is being discussed by psychologists and philosophers. The evolving story of our 'self', the way we tell about ourselves, not only creates the 'we' that we see but for some philosophers such as Paul Ricoeur helps us find a balance and justification for our choices. It helps us feel at the core of permanent gravity, despite our contradictory choices.

Via a new form of storytelling chats have radically changed not only our communication but also our way of imagining and recounting the world, and our identity. Chats have maximized what sociologists call Computer Mediated Communication (CMC), the written reproduction of verbal communication, and its resulting issues: the visual side of communication and human gestures are missing, and misunderstandings abound. To compensate this, emoticons and emojis were created. **Meanwhile, chats shape our views, our own tale of ourselves, our identity or at least the one we accredit ourselves.**

Once there were epistolary romances, only meant for poets and aristocrats. Later, love letters spread to everybody, including

CHATS HAVE TRANSFORMED OUR WAY OF IMAGINING AND RECOUNTING THE WORLD

the amazing symbol-filled compositions our illiterate emigrants would send to their distant families.

Nowadays, kids experience love via WhatsApp, most of their arguments, statements and declarations being conveyed by messages. This is a cross-class phenomenon; they build their relationship using such texts. It may seem weird to adults, even redundant, with all its constant waits. The asynchronous nature of our children's chats befuddles us. But it's totally normal to them. Popular videogame *Seen* is actually based on this. It takes place inside a Messenger-like chat, and the two leading characters are classmates Mark and Nicole. Mark's name can be changed, though, allowing me, the player, to take on his part. This way, every time Nicole writes to him, she'll write to me, and my goal is to make her fall in love with me.

In his book *Interactive Digital Narrative*, Gabriele Ferri describes *Seen* as an 'interactive narrative'.

It can be changed so that you can get endless narrative possibilities.

This is exactly why this videogame is much more appealing than other similar life-building games.

You'll find a wealth of full websites to help you with these changes, and even a Reddit channel.

After a while, users generally tend to change and create their own story, mould their own game, sometimes even mirroring their real-world exchanges with their friends.

In a chat we have the ability to pretend, much more than in person. The Internet is full of funny or serious videos showing how Instagram profiles are doped, with people trying to tell a tale of themselves that is different from reality. Every now and then a news article reminds us how people take fake selfies at home and pretend they went on a holiday.

It's hard to tell how many they are. But they exist and we all have a pathological liar among our friends.

These things used to happen even before the Internet.

Just think of when we, as kids, would brag about non-existing girlfriends or boyfriends, or when you found out that someone's 'amazing' travelling experiences were fake and the farthest place they'd ever visited was Amsterdam or London.

Those who use online dating services know how hard it is to tell whether the individuals they interact with actually adhere to their descriptions.

Back to *Seen:* Roberto Pizzato on Prismomag compares it to *Her,* Spike Jonze's 2013 movie where Theodore, who writes love letters for people who can't write, falls in love with Samantha, an artificial intelligence. She'll eventually admit she engages in the same relationship with countless other users.

Truth is surpassed by language, which shapes reality as its own liking. Just like in chats, where we create a reality we like more or that is simply more comfortable to live in.

In *Her,* Theodore's wife accuses him of not being able to relate to the real world anymore, of needing a screen that mediates reality. We could say the same of *Seen*'s Nicole, who writes to Mark instead of talking to him at school.

But if you have children you'll know that this is actually a real-life dynamics and **young people prefer chatting over talking, maybe because a screen helps overcoming embarrassment** or they're more used to look at their phones rather than at their friends' faces.

2.4 IN LOVE WITH AN **ARTIFICIAL INTELLIGENCE**

With the exponential advancement of artificial intelligence, the growth prospects of these *interactive narratives* are incalculable.

In the USA you can buy Echo, Amazon's artificial intelligence.

Echo is an odd-looking black cylinder that you keep at home and use to listen to music and as a personal assistant. It's a sort of physical static version of the PAs in our phone's operating systems, such as Siri on iOS (Apple), Google Now on Android (Google) and Cortana on Windows Phone (Microsoft). The virtual assistant inside Echo is called Alexa and works through an Internet connection, using data and information collected by Amazon.

Unlike super computers from science fiction movies, Echo comes to our houses and helps us spend our time.

You ask for a song, and it plays it. You need an alarm clock, and it sets it for you. You don't know what to wear or want to know the weather forecast for tomorrow? Alexa feeds you with this information and much more: sports results, gambling quotations, Wikipedia articles, and so on. You call out 'Alexa' and Alexa recognizes your voice. Unlike a smartphone, you cannot take it with you because it's wired. It needs an electrical outlet, so the dream of having an assistant following you around is still far to become reality. It's more like a secretary from the Fifties, taking calls for you at your office. The difference is that it doesn't need courses or work experiences to be up-to-date: Alexa operates in a cloud, so you just have to add in new features so it can evolve over time.

Why has Amazon created such an object?

First of all, because this is the future, if not the present, and it allows us to **tend on our house and control everything around us using our voice**.

According to a 2017 research by Stonetemple7, people prefer vocal searches on smartphones because they quickly provide answers and they give ad hoc answers. Not to mention the fact that typing takes time and effort, especially in our increasingly fast and bored society.

On the other hand, users often have their hands full or dirty and they don't want to screw up their valuable (of a value that is more practical than economic) smartphone.

Finally, Echo allows people to purchase products. Guess from which website? From amazon.com, of course, so that our shopping experience becomes easier, quicker and totally hassle-free. Also, investors don't really care about Jeff Bezos's company having huge turnovers but also continuous losses; its growth potential is so big that investing remains a favorable option.

The strength of Echo (and of the many products that will come after it) is its semantic engine, that allows it to learn from our answers and preferences. If you read its over 44,000 Amazon reviews – sporting an impressive 4,4 over 5 stars average ranking – you'll be astounded by the impact this product has had on the life of those who've bought it. The user reviews on Amazon's product page are quite telling.

Most of them are by registered users: real life people with a verified purchase. Some of these reviews show you how a product like Echo can change one's life. Enthusiasts are countless among those who purchased it for disabled or old people, patients with Alzheimer's, young or sick children (user Sean Kenin writes that 'Alexa has changed his son's life', who's blind from birth).

User ClemsonTiger confesses he feels bad every time he needs to say 'Alexa, stop'; while KR believes Alexa makes laziness funny; Mike H. admits he's found himself shouting 'Alexa!' to his friends when he needs something; Li thinks Echo is a more successful version of Apple's Siri; Linda has finally found a personal assistant who understands her; E. M. Foner confesses: 'before meeting Alexa I was alone' and for the sake of completeness he attaches a picture of himself sleeping with Alexa next to him; Josh Dugan thinks Alexa is 'much better than my ex'; Zak Bowles feels so much better now that he's got Alexa with him: 'I don't have to talk to myself all day anymore now: finally there's someone who listens to me'.

Newspapers from all around the world have reported that the Arkansas police has asked Amazon to provide printouts of an Echo that was purchased by the owner of a house where a murder took place. Amazon refused to oblige for privacy reasons, just like Apple did not hand the FBI the unlock codes for an iPhone belonging by the infamous San Bernardino killer. The difference, however, is that Echo records sounds and transfers them to Amazon's servers and the company processes them according to a user's requests. Amazon maintains that not everything is being recorded, but the authorities believe it may have captured something of use.

The point is that the Internet of Things (IoT) occupies an increasingly larger part of our lives, posing some interesting questions about our privacy. However, the user comments above seem to suggest that many people don't have a problem with an object that is so interconnected to their intimacy. Instead, they believe it is full of potential and a dream come true.

Echo is our first real gate to vocal interactive storytelling, and vocal interactive storytelling will be the future of our everyday life.

We won't only interact via our digital devices, but via *all* devices. The question is: will we keep on talking to our friends and neighbors or will we act like Josh Dugan and end up interacting with a home object that tells us his stories – some made up, some taken from the Internet – and listens to our useless thoughts all day long?

Italians will discover the effect of Echo quite late, because of semantics. Siri is still far from perfect, but it will eventually improve. These tools will change the life of all users, with increasingly less tactile use and more voice recognition technology. Not to mention all the inevitable privacy issues: today we give away our clicks to be recognized, one day we'll give away our thoughts. So far, privacy issues have revolved around credit cards and clicks, but one day they'll encompass all aspects of our lives, which will be stored on a server on the other side of the world.

One day, Echo will be outshined too. Amazon was only disruptive in the eBook segment with its Kindle because Google and Apple essentially gave up because they could not sell apps for Kindles. Every time Amazon has launched a supposedly new breakthrough device (such as the Kindle Fire, its smartphone, or Chromecast) it was quickly surpassed by its competitors.

2.5 HOW MAJORS ARE DICTATING THE **NEW RULES FOR ADVERTISING**

Every now and then, a controversy about Facebook advertising breaks out.

Advertisers drool over data, they invest to increase the visibility of their posts, they pay analysts to read all the reports. As it turns out, these data are usually incorrect. Companies complain, disapprove, schedule meetings but Mr. Zuckerberg doesn't seem to worry much.

Those who pay ask for reliable figures. But figures don't necessarily mean satisfaction. Apparently, on Facebook you pay for ads even if users view them for zero seconds. This has impacted the minimum amount set forth by the Interactive Advertising Bureau (IAB). As for standard ads, it required 50% of an ad pixels to be visible in the browser window for one second. A scant second is nothing compared to a 25-second TV commercial, which also fills up the whole screen. As for larger ads, the 1-second requirement was for 30% of an ad pixels; as for videos, 50% for 2 seconds. However, Facebook begs to differ and clearly stated that a user swiping his finger on a smartphone screen and skipping the ad altogether is a good enough minimum requirement and the advertiser must pay for it as if it had been viewed. During the 2016 Business Insider's Ignition in New York, Facebook Vice President

Andrew Bosworth admitted that a real person watching an ad for zero seconds counts as an impression.

The question is: will advertisers rebel and leave Facebook? They won't, because they can't. Facebook is made of people, it's made for them and people love to be on it, so Facebook's point is more or less as follows: 'This is my place and this is my audience, and I'm lending you two billion users. What are you going to do? Play by my rules or try and reach your target some other way?' Nobody will ever leave and a total boycott is inconceivable, since Facebook provides a highly accurate service that no other sales channel can give.

According to Drew Huening, Director at Omnicom Media Group's Accuen, there will be no decrease in advertising investments: if advertisers are satisfied with their ads being watched for a split millisecond, it's the advertising market that needs to change, not Facebook that must adapt. Also, the costs of Facebook campaigns are so cheap that they're totally worthwhile. Also, all social media are fighting against bots and ignorant DYI advertisers. They know that if advertisers have no return, they won't come back.

That's why they keep on suggesting the best target audiences, the best copies, the best pictures and so on. Sometimes they even automatically change a selected target audience if their algorithms deem it as wrong.

In other words, the 'new' platforms have reshaped the advertising world and may even take the advertising agencies' place, with the goal of ensuring the satisfaction of advertisers.

Media are people, after all. And they need to survive.

2.6 BLOCKCHAIN, THE 'NEXT BIG THING' THAT WILL CHANGE THE MARKETING WORLD

For many, Blockchain is a synonym for bitcoin, the controversial digital currency that is often associated with scandals and uncontrolled speculations. Those who have heard about it, deem it as a thing for geeks or maybe banks and technologic finance. The truth, however, is that it may bring about some interesting developments in many fields, especially marketing.

To be honest, this is due to the fact that this technology is complex, difficult to understand and anything but intuitive.

To put it down simply, a Blockchain decentralizes and neutralizes the role of any central authority, be it monetary or any other kind, by means of peer-to-peer file sharing protocols, public- and private-key cryptography and hash encryptions, which transform variable length data into fixed length records using a unique encryption key.

In simpler words this means that every piece of data or record, for example in a transaction, is logged and synchronized on all the network nodes (computers) in an encrypted form and all data must match on all nodes. Otherwise, the action is not authorized. Data are the 'transactions', the blocks are the logs of how and when the transactions are indelibly entered.

The identity of who generated the transaction is public, while the type of transaction is concealed.

Data are not modifiable in any way. If someone tries to tamper with a block, all the blocks that come next are invalidated and the change is automatically removed from the network.

This process has not prevented frauds, however.

It's a technology that can still be fine-tuned.

Theoretically, the Blockchain architecture can be applied to any type of digital data, from bitcoins to medical records, from contracts to media.

It could radically change the whole digital marketing industry and bring significant benefits to those who work on the Web.

It is a 'distributed ledger' that can keep 'non-hackerable' tracks of transactions and store a record of people's digital signatures.

The fact that a central authority (Google or Facebook, but also a notary or a public official) that acts as a guarantor and judge for the soundness of the operation is no longer needed makes the relationship between parties – for instance a marketer who wants to post an ad and a website owner – more direct. Basically, if the Blockchain can verify that every user is a real user and can also validate the reliability of the real clicks a website manager requests a payment for, the advertiser and the website can make a deal with no middle-person. This translates to less expenses and more earnings for both parties and maybe a better control over results, as we discussed above.

For instance, Microsoft is working on a Blockchain-based identification method to prevent online frauds and fight software piracy. 'Once you have registered your identity in the Blockchain, its self-sovereign nature becomes an asset belonging to the individual, allowing him to operate in many scenarios for the time needed by the parties involved and based on the information required' says Yorke Rhodes III, Microsoft's Blockchain Business Strategist.

Online frauds, even in advertising, amount to about 6 or 7 billion dollars every year. Removing this squander would automatically lead to an increase in marketers' earnings and a bigger share of money that can be invested in digital advertising, ultimately benefiting the market. The problem is that marketing has shown no interest in this matter and another four or five years will pass before it happens. Applications are also very limited: one is BitTeaser, a Danish advertising network that uses Blockchain to collect advertising revenue using bitcoins instead of money. Despite a system that is slow in sensing this change taking place, Blockchain is really 'the next big thing', a turning point for marketing, and this is especially true for multimedia publishing and digital advertising. Since the Blockchain bypasses central authorities and cuts all intermediation costs, it also favors micro transactions. This may open a new route for developing new content fruition modes and new earning scenarios.

For instance, publishers may allow readers to enjoy an ad-free page at the cost of a cent or less. Or they may grant access to their websites only to those who pay a risible subscription fee. As for the advertisers, they would probably be keen to paying more to grab advertising spaces with safer returns than today.

Blockchain also allows you to check the authenticity of products. In October 2016, during the Shanghai Fashion Week, Babyghost used VeChain's Blockchain platform to let customers test the authenticity of a range of bags by scanning tags with their smartphones. By doing so, they would retrace a bag's full history: its designer, the factory where it had been manufactured, who had made it, and so on. This is great for preventing forgery, it helps the company develop a tighter relationship with customers and acts as a better advertising drive than any traditional system we're used to. It also allows to carefully manage sales data, while protecting customer privacy.

Looking at the Blockchain from a marketing perspective, I believe the proper question we should ask to any brand in any industry is the following: 'Considering the benefits this technology provides, which new uses can be developed and how can you take advantage of it for the good of both your business and customers?'. A proper answer needs to be found.

Let's dispel another myth: the Blockchain isn't only suitable for finance. If you need a safe public ledger and a way to confirm the real identity of its participants, this tool is for you.

Think of healthcare, where data confidentiality and identity protection are a very sensible and crucial matter.

This technology may help us safely store a patient's sensible data and hospitals are actually thinking of a way to use it. It would be groundbreaking, especially in Italy, a country where the digitalization of archives has been discussed for twenty years but no hospital can yet access a 3-month-old digital X-ray image taken at another facility.

For instance, BitHealth is a Blockchain-based healthcare system: user data are distributed across the world using a peer-to-peer file sharing tool similar to BitTorrent.

Medical records are encrypted so a doctor only needs to retrieve a record to know everything about a patient: visits, surgeries, pain locations, medications, exams. The patient's name is not displayed, though: everything is kept anonymous.

This way different doctors can evaluate a case and share their opinions, even if they live in different countries.

Their services are then paid using bitcoins, after all digital signatures are approved.

This allows clinical record to be easily shared among multiple doctors, and the variations of the unnamed patient's condition can be used for a consultation about the most suitable treatment or the collection of data for a scientific research.

Recently, IBM Watson Health and the Food and Drug Administration (FDA) have signed an agreement for the establishment of a safe, efficient and scalable exchange method for healthcare data – electronic medical records, trials and tests, genomics data, and so on – using a Blockchain.

In the early stages, IBM and the FDA will focus on oncologic data and exchanges will be mediated by the owner of such data, that is the patient. Data will also be generated from smart watches and wearable technology in general, Internet of Things devices, tablets and smartphones.

One example is AppleHealth, an iPhone app that helps users monitor their health and sends their vital data to researchers using the ResearchKit application. This huge and one-of-a-kind *knowledge base* is powered by the latest Apple product: the Apple Watch. **What data will**

be collected? Heart pulses, arrhythmias, heart deficiencies. People are media.

Always and anyway.

Thanks to the Blockchain technology, hospitals may benefit from a global, synched and shared network, updated with real time data about a patient's admission to a hospital, wherever it occurs. And the patient would always be aware of how information is handled.

Let's now move to another field: music.

We think Spotify is so amazing, and we thought the same of Napster in the past. But what about the future? In late 2015, British singer Imogen Heap used the Blockchain to establish a direct communication with her fans and release her song *Tiny Human* with all associated data. 'The Blockchain allows you to link a specific file to its payment by means of a digital wallet. In my case, when somebody listens to one of my songs, they can decide if they want to purchase it right away' she stated.

In other words, a user must not wait for the distribution or release times of a track and the artist immediately receives payment with no intermediation.

There's also a new platform called Bitshares aiming at bringing singers, songwriters, bands and users together via a technology-verified interaction during the whole process of creating a song. Musicians can share their repertoires and music lovers can support and promote them. Digital music can be available everywhere, at any moment and on any platform.

This process gets rid of intermediation and can also be applied to online videogames: if players have one verified identity, their information and activities can be transferred across different games, regardless of the platforms they use.

Since it allows the monitoring and management of a secure, efficient, irrefutable and fraud-proof identity, the Blockchain technology proves to be useful for many sectors. It may drastically change how a municipality network (for birth, residency, marriage documents, and so on) or a contract works.

One day it may even replace notaries.

'Smart contracts' between private parties are legally binding digital agreements that are directly negotiated by both parties without a notary, a lawyer or a bank and allow the contracting parties a certain level of freedom in setting forth the contract terms.

If, for any reason (a sale of a motorbike, the payment of an installment, a mortgage, and so on) 'subject A' wants to pay 1,000 Euros to 'subject B' but only under certain conditions and at a specific time, his funds will only be released when such conditions are fulfilled. Or, if a clearing company is appointed to perform two operations a week, payments a

authorized after the system certifies that the clearing staff has accessed

the premises on the agreed dates and times.

Both sides can neither cheat nor rip each other off, because Blockchain

records cannot be tampered with, as they're fully automated and

indelibly logged inside the Blockchain itself.

Entrepreneur and Blockchain researcher Bettina Warburg explains it so

well: 'Blockchains allows the creation of an open and global platform

we can use to log any attestation about any individual from any source.

This allows the creation of a portable and controlled identity for a user'.

Platforms such as Ethereum are making smart contracts a reality and

already store a number of logged valid contracts.

2.7 INDUSTRY 4.0 AND RULING BY PLATFORMS

Digital technology is totally disruptive, it breaks every pattern.
Let's say you're an engineer and you invented an algorithm for
driverless trucks that's way more efficient than Google's.
You'll found a company that is qualitatively better than Google or any
other transport company because you can bring down logistic costs,
since no human factor involved and timings and fuel costs are
streamlined. The only operations left are goods load-ins and load-outs,
but a smart robot can easily handle them. UPS or TNT will come
knocking at your door and offer a huge amount of money to buy your
algorithm, before the damage you've done to them becomes
devastating. If they don't quickly adapt, they will close shop.
Two young American companies, dyapers.com (diapers) and soap.com
(washing and cleaning products), have made quite an impression lately.
Some may object: 'Don't parents have time to buy diapers?'. Of course
they do, but not all Americans live in urban centers and shopping at a
mall is like a 'self-punishment trip' for them. Also, if they forget to buy
something it can be a real nightmare, because they're hours away from
a store selling diapers. dyapers.com is just perfect for these people:
great assortment, suitable delivery times and fair prices. That's why it

was a success. Amazon bought them out, because dyapers.com was stronger than Amazon in the diaper sector. Did the creators of both websites rest on their laurels? Not at all. They moved on and invented a 'bundle' system for purchases: when customers step into a store, an algorithm combines all available discounts based on what they put in their shopping carts. The more they buy, the more discounts they get. Needless to say, it was another big breakthrough. Walmart bought it out.

In other words, if you let your guard down, you'll be surpassed and slaughtered. Global companies might go: 'We'll buy these youngsters out, so we're safe.' But 'these youngsters' will take their money and come back with something new and stronger. They're called digital start-ups.

Before the advent of digital technology you could not do something like this with no money.

Potentially, digital technology allows anybody to make great achievements, and it never sleeps.

Technology has always overturned the labor market: it scares those who fear their craft may disappear, it allures the younger generations who feel more at ease with more innovative jobs, it is interesting for employers who learn they can produce more while

paying less.

This still happens today, and in an exaggerated form, because people believe that robots will take every job from human beings. And figures confirm that a general worker will soon be just a memory.

In post-war USA one worker out of three was employed in manufacturing. In 2017, it's one out of eleven.

Experts confirm our perception will change and there's very little we can do about it, except finding training alternatives for the younger generations so that they're ready for the new market or at least can find assistance if they can't find some room in it.

The new industry is called Industry 4.0.

Let's start from the name: 4.0 is the fourth stage in a development that began long ago, in the steam power days.

In Industry 4.0, manufacturing is handled by machines and automated and interconnected tools that rely on data for their operation.

The rise of Industry 1.0 dates back to the XVIII century, when steam power was first used to operate machines replacing the scarce power sources that were used at the time: nature elements (water, wind, and so on) and human or animal muscles.

We then moved to Industry 2.0 (which has nothing to do with Web 2.0) and the introduction of oil and electricity and the Ford model of mass production: the assembly line.

It marks the dawn of the market as we know it, with serial products and people who buy them without standing on ceremony if their neighbors own the same things, because they're happy to own more stuff at an affordable price.

The next level, and our last as of today, is Industry 3.0. It means IT, computers, programming machines via other machines. A lot of manual labor disappears and automation is applied to organization. Those who are good at learning how a screen and keyboard work easily make a career.

Today we're about to get to the next stage. We're on the verge of a Matrix-like scenario, with machines taking the place of humans and crushing them all. Who knows, it may really be like that.

For now, machines are still under human control, but humans have a multitude of tiny helpers: sensors.

Industry 4.0 is filled with sensors that log everything. The whole manufacturing process is controlled, items are scanned, stages are supervised by sensors. This results in significant time savings.

Errors are less and less, checks can be performed where the human eye can't reach, sometimes for its own safety.

None of us would expect a worker standing 2 inches away from a milling machine to make sure a cut is properly done.

Sensors don't only work along the assembly line, they're also integrated in final products. Inside a jet plane, components immediately report tampering or malfunctioning, while the outside shell monitors weather conditions. Everything will be monitored to avoid malfunctioning. Data will become crucial, along with data mining. Human beings, machines and objects for smart system management are and will be increasingly connected in real time.

Industry 4.0 was born and spread in Germany, a country which, despite its relatively small size and the China's aggressive competition, is still at the vanguard of the manufacturing industry. China is not watching from a distance, though, as their 10-year investment plan is actually focusing on these very developments. According to consultancy firm Roland Berger, if Europe invested 60 billion Euros every year until 2030, 6 million qualified jobs would be made, since the EU hires 150,000 experts a year in IT alone. These experts are needed to manage networks and create 'smart' appliances such as fridges notifying you when food is about to expire or run out, what you should buy (maybe one day it will even buy itself), all the while providing data and numbers to the manufacturer.

We cannot accurately predict which and how many objects will be connected to each other and to humans. According to Gartner, today they're 6.4 billion and they will be 20.8 billion in 2020. The Internet of Things Trend Report by DHL and Cisco predicts a 50 billion figure, with a 8,000 billion dollar value in the next 10 years: 2.1 trillion dollars in innovation and manufacturing plants, 1.9 trillion dollars in supply chains, 1.2 trillion dollars in increased productivity, 700 billion dollars in extra services and customer satisfaction.

Introducing digital technology in a company is a huge change; for many it's like a fourth industrial revolution that will replace not only repetitive manual labor but also (and for the first time) intellectual labor. Meanwhile,

HUMAN BEINGS, MACHINES AND OBJECTS ARE AND WILL BE INCREASINGLY CONNECTED IN REAL TIME

many stages can already be easily replaced.

One example of this may be Easyjet. Every time a plane lands, its fuselage must be thoroughly inspected before the aircraft can take off again.

The inspection is performed by eye by specialized engineers and sometimes by the pilot himself: they go around the aircraft and check if anything is out of place, if any dangerous crack is present, if all screws and bolts are in place, and so on.

This inspection takes place before every take-off and, in order to reduce waiting times and operating costs, Easyjet uses a drone.

The drone flies around the aircraft, scans its whole surface and compares it against a set of standard default parameters stored in its memory. If you don't think about lost jobs, this application is an example of how companies can benefit from digital technology on various levels: money savings, time savings (which actually mean saving money in terms of aircrafts ground stops), efficiency increases and security improvements.

The most common mistake Italian companies do when dealing with digital technology is to think it's all about having a website. But everybody has a website today, even the smallest perfume shop in the smallest town, and sometimes it is even better than a lot of corporate websites. But it's not a website that makes a company 'digital'. Anyone can have a 'shopping cart' today: Google allows you to create your own website, another company sells you the ability to enable a shopping cart. You can even start up an e-commerce business by yourself with just a few thousand Euros and start selling whatever you want, without needing much else.

B2B businesses haven't still figured out what to do, while B2C businesses only tend to focus on their websites. This lack of openness is the reason why the Italian government has put so much emphasis on Industry 4.0 in recent times: companies tend to purchase a piece of equipment instead of figuring out how innovation can improve their business efficiency. This way they'll never understand that they need to change. Think about telemetry: it can hugely grow if digital technology is used to control production metrics and workers' actions. Let's assume your business manufactures self-finished products, such as rebars: monitoring is performed by optical sensors but you can also implement a digital scanning process that not only ensures every single rebar is perfect, but also captures it and stores it. In the unfortunate event a final user sues you for whatever malfunctioning reason, you'll have pictures, analyses and specific characteristics of that peculiar rebar in your database and you'll be able fight back in court quite easily. Similarly, a manufacturer specializing in disk brakes can prove that a car accident was caused by product wear or other external factors and not by a manufacturing defect.

In a Capital magazine interview, Carlo Calenda, Italian Minister of Economic Development during both Matteo Renzi's and current Gentiloni's governments, has summarized the benefits of Industry 4.0 as follows: robotics and advanced automation **reduce errors, timings**

and costs and improve productivity and safety; the supply chain becomes shorter; high connectivity can take advantage of UWB (Ultra-Wide Band); the processing and analysis of huge amounts of data with increasingly lower costs allow for better decisions and estimates about production and energy consumption and helps developing systems that provide customized and immediate feedbacks to consumers; scale production of small quantities is enabled; digital contact with customers, sometimes through augmented reality (visors are already on the market), allows for the collection of feedbacks and orientations and extends post-sale services.

However, while incorporating microchips is easy, analyzing them is a much harder task.

Most of all, it's crucial that we learn how to use them, because – as it sometimes happens with user data – the risk of confining them in PowerPoint slideshows is just around the corner. Henning Kagermann, head of Acatech, believes that 'whoever controls the platforms will rule the future'. All the big companies want their systems installed in smart IoT objects.

The Apple system on Ferrari cars is worth an astounding amount of data for Tim Cook's company, and many others are starting to realize that such data are a godsend and the information they provide is worth real money.

To lose your 'sovranity' over these data means you will miss the future. It means you'll become like Android smartphone manufacturers who hand over all data to Google.

2.8 THE NEW STATE: **HYPER-CONTROL** VS. **HYPER-PARTICIPATION**

My mobile phone can be remote-controlled, its microphone can be activated unbeknown to me.

My computer camera can be switched on and used to film me without me even noticing.

Sure, I can meet with my friends at an isolated location and bring no devices so that we can't be reached. But it would be useless anyway. Once back home, our behaviors would be verifiable: we'd leave some unmistakable traces about our lives and our intentions behind. An algorithm would be able to realize that the four of us are connected, that we're plotting something and that we must be put under surveillance.

This is exactly what is happening, but very few have realized.

Our emails are stored on the other side of the planet, we're monitored and they know everything we think. They've read it, they still do.

Sophisticated algorithms that can read, predict and respond don't exist yet, but they soon will.

In five years. Ten, at most.

I think of what the UNO could do with such a tool. But I also see the downside to this. The problem with Europe is that it hasn't developed a counter-platform. We have nothing in place, we've allowed ourselves to be conquered.

People go: 'How bad are these Chinese folks who won't let Google and Facebook in'. But in China they know better, they actually got it before everybody else. Their answer was: 'When we're ready, we'll make a counter-Google and we'll be very good at it'. And in the end they actually made it, it's called Baidu. So now Google's major competitor is in Beijing.

China wants no Trojan horses and neither does Russia, to the extent that the founder of the biggest Russian social platform, Vkontakte, went on exile. Pavel Durov was fired from his own company after accusing the government of requesting confidential information about the organizers of an anti-Russia rally in Kiev.

There are tools that can read what I read, see what I see, learn what I have bought, my musical, artistic and sexual preferences. All of this was impossible in the past.

If I talked to a friend nobody would know except for the two of us. I could buy anything and it would go untraced. I could flee (and even remain in Italy or Europe) and nobody would find out – nor had the tools to find out – where I had gone.

There's a show called 'Chi l'ha visto?' on Italian TV, which helps finding missing people. The only way I can be featured on that show today is to become a homeless, and it may be not enough. To truly disappear, I should leave everything behind and abandon the civil society. Otherwise I'll be found somehow. My only alternative is a life of deprivation in the middle of the Amazon forest, where I'll probably be dead in a couple of weeks after a spider bites me. When I look around, I only see people sporting the same haircut, the same waxed eyebrows and the same beard, taking the same pictures, walking the same dog. All of them are alike.

As usual, Woody Allen comes to mind in these cases. In his movie *Midnight in Paris* he proves we're all nostalgic for a past we haven't lived and we easily idealize. Looking-alike men have always existed, as René Magritte's paintings suggest with their thousands of gray men raining from the sky, in the past, in a city like London citizens were all identical: a woman looking for her husband would have gone crazy because she couldn't have told one from the other all wearing the same bowler hat and smoking the same pipe.

Today, digital technology makes individuals feel like they have a bullhorn in their hands and they can speak, build an identity and know things.

In terms of means, media were only one-way once: somebody else would write a newspaper and we would read it, TV stations would broadcast a show and we would watch it.

THERE ARE TOOLS THAT CAN LEARN ALL MY MUSICAL, ARTISTIC AND SEXUAL PREFERENCES

Interactions were null, sometimes radios would put the occasional phone call on air, and that was that. Today, the power of sending a message is in everybody's hands. People have always used some 'people type' of communication, such as the revolts, rallies and in recent times strikes.

But media have changed and the fact that we're poorer, angrier, more embittered but also permanently connected allows people to express ourselves every day, for better or worse.

Online newspapers host comments by readers, and the thing that strikes me the most is how low their level of comprehension is.

The vast majority of people don't understand what an article really says and, without being judgmental, the majority of comments are totally pointless and ridiculous.

It's like a bullhorn for nothingness. You can hear the voice of those who would have remained silent in the past.

It's not yet clear whether this 'bullhorn capability' actually affects the collectivity. We have recently witnessed one of the biggest financial crises in history: huge scandals sparkling discussions, pushing people to throw bricks at bank presidents who were guilty of wasting huge amounts of money and yet got other-worldly bonuses. All of that while workers with 1,000 Euro salaries were forced to pay off the banks' debts. Had this happened in the Seventies, people would have probably reached for their guns.

We have an amazing array of possibilities when it comes to receiving information, and we get to know things in zero time. If anything happens at 8 p.m., the whole world immediately learns about it. So people are media, but what's their influence?

Is this amplification a way to let everybody pour out their anger or frustration and level it? In the USA, boycotters actually boycott, while in Italy we change our indignation targets or enemies overnight.

While we almost get angry on cue, somebody else keeps on making money. I'm talking about those who log everything we do, from our interactions to our car trips. They make and sell almost anything, partly thanks to us.

They get more and more relevant and rich. But we're the ones who should get that money, probably.

The dystopian future envisioned by George Orwell (and Dave Eggers in *The Circle* or Jonathan Franzen in *Purity*) may never become a reality, but we should bear in mind that we have exchanged our ethics for a capitalistic model that doesn't belong to us.

We weren't born to *make and buy*: this mechanism was only ignited in the most recent time of human life on Earth.

Our society *makes* and *buys*, ceaselessly. There's no reason not to assume that a social change may eventually come, because digital technology helps us develop a new self-consciousness and we'll start wondering why we must live in this type of society. For now, many are still only asking the question and haven't found any alternative answer.

According to recent data, human workforce is being rapidly replaced by equipment. We won't be makers and consumers anymore. We'll only be consumers, because robots will become the makers. But if a computer starts making things in my place, I will probably stop buying.

There's no reason to assume that the production and consumption chain will forever be what manufacturers (of cars, phones and anything else) want it to be. One day, we may refrain from replacing our devices only because a button is relocated every six months, or operating power is slightly increased or a new feature is added.

As a matter of fact, however, in recent years the system has increasingly been about the *buying* and less about the *making*.

There's a city where every paradigm we know is changing in this very moment: Singapore.

Most Westerners have never visited Singapore and wouldn't probably be able to locate it on a map. They'll easily mistake it for Shanghai or an Arab city in the middle of a desert, like Dubai.

This book isn't about geography, though: Singapore is interesting because it's trying to think about the future. It's much more than a 'smart city': it's actually a 'data city'. Derrick de Kerckhove – Scientific Director of Italian magazine 'Media2000', Director of the 'TuttiMedia' Observatory at the Beijing Internet Forum and Director of the McLuhan Program in Culture and Technology in Toronto from 1983 until 2008 – has a term for this: *datacracy*, 'a form of civilization based on data, apparently allowing us to live in an ideal place with no robberies and theft, and so much more'.

In the era of micro-cellular terrorism, with very small groups performing scattered and self-organized attacks, control by machines may become popular in places like Paris or Tunis and meet their demand for safety.

The term datacracy (power of data) conveys the risks of a possible drift: 'Leaders are made by an algorithm, citizens comply to social behaviors imposed by technology, the state apparatus goes from organic to technical, with governments that will tend to use technology to control the ongoing change process as well'.

'A sort of soft tyranny that can gradually bring us to the ruling by machines' de Kerckhove warns us. The citizens of Singapore, just like most of us, spend a lot of their lives in front of a screen and leave many traces behind: they're geo-located and what they write and say is constantly acquired.

Institutions are wholly relying on these data in order to improve people's lives. If many people take the train at around five o'clock, then it's safe to schedule a train at that time. If there are too many cars on a road and a traffic jam is forming, a central super brain system blocks all accesses and imposes a toll to invite drivers to pick another route. This way everything is smoother, nicer, tidier, and life is faster and safer.

Since its foundation, the city state of Singapore has focused on one of the essential rules for most Asian people: order.

For city founder Lee Kuan Yew, this was particularly necessary in order to control the disputes among the four different ethnic groups that live here. This equilibrium is based on two technologies: a smartphone, that stays with an individual all day every day for even the tiniest activity, and a special ID card that holds the individual's personal data. Except for the ID card, this is what happens all over the planet: phones are omnipresent in people's hands or pockets, they're something we can't deprive ourselves of.

What would we do without it? What if someone calls us? What if someone writes to us? Even if nobody actually ever does, our friends may post something on Facebook and we may miss the coolest event of the month!

But phones have actually changed *all* our habits: if we need to find a place, we won't ask for direction, we'll turn on our Google Maps GPS option. The same applies when it comes to bus timetables, purchasing train tickets or calling a taxi.

As a recent Italian movie, *Perfetti sconosciuti (Perfect Strangers)* by director Paolo Genovese, points out, our mobile phone holds every single information about us, sometimes at our own expense.

Meanwhile, Edward Snowden's leak from the NSA has confirmed what experts already knew: anyone can access our phones quite effortlessly and without legal legitimacy. In the past, we used to be quite discreet about our upcoming holidays because we were afraid of burglars, now those of us who cheat on their partners keep their chat conversations a click away and we all carry a geo-locator in our pocket. Not to mention when we share our location on purpose, by posting a picture on Facebook. **In Singapore technology makes life easier but increases monitoring. However, citizens are not shocked about it and actually appreciate it.** If you lose your wallet you'll easily find it, because cameras will know where it is and who took it. Trains are always on time, in Singapore.

Authorities have even prevented a rape by analyzing the whereabouts of a suspect: an algorithm had recognized the man's face and reported him as dangerous.

Control by technologies makes us safer, until we ask ourselves who's controlling them and why. Those who know how things work in Singapore know that the price for reassurance is restriction. As a matter of fact, the teen version of myself used to break most Singapore common rules: do not spit, do not chew gum in the open, flush the toilet in public restrooms, no graffiti, no vandalism, no porn, no homosexuality, no nudity at home except when you're in the bathroom. Those who complain get in trouble. Singapore is full of 'regime bloggers', very well-known influencers who teach good manners and respect for the rules. Others, such as 16-year-old blogger Amos Yee, go to jail for criticizing the government. All media are controlled. The 'ruling by algorithms' infuses a sense of harmony to justice as well. All collected information becomes data, which in turn are used to impose sanctions. Thousands of Smart National Platform (SNP) cameras have replaced politicians and judges, and citizens seem to appreciate the new order.

Experts believe that many citizens censor themselves without even noticing. They don't want to take chances. They all believe it's a price worth paying.

Will these technologies make our lives better or will they shut us off? Will we need to control them or is Singapore a typically Asian phenomenon, where maintaining law and order is one of the state's tasks, as opposed to the Western dream of freedom? These are questions we ought to ask ourselves.

In this regard, De Kerckhove quotes Marshall McLuhan, who couldn't obviously predict the Internet and yet was already pessimistic: 'Electrical information devices for universal, tyrannical womb-to tomb surveillance are causing a very serious dilemma between our claim to privacy and the community's need to know. The older, traditional ideas of private, isolated thoughts and actions — the patterns of mechanistic technologies — are very seriously threatened by new methods of instantaneous electric information retrieval, by the electrically computerized dossier bank — that one big gossip column that is unforgiving, unforgetful and from which there is no redemption, no erasure of early 'mistakes.' We have already reached a point where remedial control, born out of knowledge of media and their total effects on all of us, must be exerted.'

Chapter 3
PAYING IN 'LIKES'

3.1 WHAT'S BEHIND A **'LIKE'?**

3.2 SOCIAL CHANNELS AND **BUSINESSES**

3.3 CHATBOTS

3.4 WHAT'S NEXT?

3.1 WHAT'S BEHIND A 'LIKE'?

The activity of an average Facebook user is based on one thing and one thing only, getting 'Likes', and it applies to everything, from the things we write to the pictures we post.

A 'Like' is a social platform's currency (and as such it holds a quantified and quantifiable economic value). People do not 'Like' an uncool car brand, they 'Like' luxury models such as a Ferrari, Maserati or BMW.

Similarly, they post pictures of dinners featuring a rather popular acquaintance or a hot friend in a tight dress, not their lunch breaks with a coworker sporting some sweaty armpits, an ugly colleague who clearly has no mirrors at home or someone at a nearby table at war with a forkful of spaghetti.

The same happens to me, when I decide to show what I like or am interested in. Even though I'm into all kinds of stuff, I choose to post just one thing and avoid sharing much else. I happen to watch the occasional bad taste video but I'm ashamed to let other people know, because I'd look foolish in my coworkers' eyes. Or I do the exact opposite: I may share the video because I love to look like I'm a carefree guy, but I won't repost a technical document about the latest breakthroughs in steel resistance because none of my friends would get it, even if I have thoroughly discussed it at work.

The truth is I look for consensus, just like everybody else. I long for some 'Likes', I even accept to take pity on myself in order to get them. In fact, playing the victim is the strategy I love to adopt sometimes.

Consensus is always good. If I get a hundred 'Likes' for writing 'What a loser I am!', I'm fine with that. I'm fine because it works.

We've already covered Antoine Garrot's story, the guy who decided to make a social experiment that can actually destroy relationships: he replied to Facebook posts by only telling the truth.

Needless to say, he lost half of his Facebook friends and probably just as many offline.

In real life you don't go around showing pictures where you play the clown and embarrass yourself. And if you do, your friends will never congratulate with you. But that's what happens on Facebook most of the times. Hard-to-watch scenes are regularly covered in compliments and heart emotes. Can't we recognize clumsiness and ugliness anymore? Of course we can, but we're acting in a rambling way for the simplest of reasons: *quid pro quo*. I make a compliment to you so you'll return it to me.

This is how Mr. Zuckerberg has changed the semantics of the term 'friends': he's actually given a new meaning to it and transformed everything that revolves around it. **Let's be honest: if they had asked us to name our friends before Facebook, we would've listed from three to ten names, maybe thirty if we're extremely sociable people. Before Facebook, none of us would have rattled off 500 names.**

Oh, there's a way of calling our friends in real life, by the way. It's *real friends*. And yes, it's just as simple as that.

The point is that Facebook is *not* our real life; on Facebook we show a character, an avatar. That's why I have a nice picture of myself on my profile, and not one showing my ordinary everyday appearance. And even if I'm not good-looking in it, at least it's a picture that I'm proud of for some reason.

If I have dinner at Gordon Ramsey's restaurant I'll promptly post about it, but I won't post anything if I'm having some canned tuna. Nobody will ever know about it. Our life on Facebook is a parallel existence, a lie. That's why we always make a distinction between our life and our 'real life', our friends andour 'real friends', us and 'the real us'. It's exhausting, frankly. Let's get back to me, to the things I do online.

If I can make a witty comment on a friend's post or say something funny because I'm good at wordplays, I will so that my friends know they have me, brilliant and smart-mouthed, as a friend.

But if I can't think of anything funny to post, well, I won't post anything. If I was face to face with the same friend, I would probably be ashamed of saying nothing and my

FACEBOOK IS NOT OUR REAL LIFE, ON FACEBOOK WE SHOW A CHARACTER, AN AVATAR

silence would vouch for my dislike for the thing he's just said. 'Myself' on Facebook is not me, it's the 'me' I wish I always was, and which I allow myself to be for a few seconds a day.

Facebook is a huge make-believe and it is based on two major strategies.

The first is that it never tells you who viewed your profile. LinkedIn does so, but LinkedIn is a social network for professionals and those who reach my user profile apparently do it for scouting purposes. Facebook is different. We all use it at least once a day to learn what a particular individual is doing, where and with whom. We read the things he or she writes and we keep an eye on who 'Likes' or comments him or her. Who is this guy? What does she want from him? What's his job? And we go deeper and deeper, learning things about a total stranger who has simply 'Liked' someone we know or care about.

I'm pretty sure that one day I will be busier than usual and miss an email informing me that Facebook has started sending notifications like LinkedIn, allowing people to know who visited their profiles. Sooner or later this thing will happen, but I won't realize and I'll embarrass myself.

Facebook's second strategic factor is its lack of a 'Dislike' button. Mr. Zuckerberg doesn't want it, at all (who can vouch that his opinion won't change in the future though?).

What would happen if there was one such button? We can only guess, but I fear it may spark witch hunts, literally. That's because we tend to like one thing and dislike one hundred. Our 'Dislikes' may lead to actual online wars between opposing music fan bases or supporters of different behaviors or ideas. The impact would be huge. A 'Dislike' button would help save some time, though, because I'd stop creating fake profiles to say what I really mean. But many users don't have secondary profiles and experience Facebook for what it is: a place where they can release their pressures and frustrations, a place where yelling is the rule.

But I'm a part of the civil society and I cannot afford such carefree behavior, at least not in my real name. So I troll my way in!

The core of this phenomenon is – and will always be – *digital*

narcissism, something all social media live and prosper upon.

In the name of neo narcissism we do things offline so that we can be 'Liked' online. One day the most valued currency may well be a 'Like', a new principle to assess our reputation, just as it happens _Black Mirror's Nosedive_, a chilling piece of television where everybody smiles to get high ratings from the people they interact with.

3.2 SOCIAL CHANNELS AND BUSINESSES

When I 'Like' a snack on a social network, its company will feed me with contents every day. If I'm not interested in them, I won't look at them or I'll stop following the page. If I never look at them, after a while the algorithms will stop displaying them. This is the boring everyday life we're used to.

The watchword for a business on social networks should be: 'what's our role and position?'. Let's face it: some companies have very tedious and irrelevant Facebook profiles. They just tell about themselves and their business. They fill their pages with products and offers, as if their followers were always eager and ready to purchase from them. Others just keep talking about their organizational processes, which I don't really care about.

According to some, the problem lies in the fact that social networks are actually 'social networks' (pun intended) where people meet, chat, even argue. If businesses want to join in and have their say, they must refrain from simply advertising their stuff and start encouraging conversations, confrontations and discussions.

I have a much more critical approach: it really bugs me when a post I don't care about bothers me while I'm on my phone, minding my own business, taking a break in the bathroom or relaxing on my sofa. I simply don't want to see it. I wish I could unfriend some obnoxious people, let alone the companies that post things about themselves or their latest products. I only bear with them because I know they allow Facebook to be free (of charge). But how annoying they are!

There's another way I can interact with brands on social platforms, however, and it is to release my anger, whether I have a reason for it or I'm simply looking for my next scapegoat, something or someone to pillory. Let's be honest: this is what most people are actually looking forward to.

So let me introduce you to the two most typical scenarios of CRM (Customer Relations Management, which we'll discuss more thoroughly in the next paragraph and in Chapter 5) in the digital era: one is a customer who's found a piece of iron in his snack and the other is somebody who goes after random targets. (If you do that in real life and shout at a friend out of context, he will most probably slap you in the face and tell everybody you're an anti-social freak who makes a fuss for no reason.) Let's start from the first scenario: someone complaining about something that has actually happened. Companies can't even think about not replying, otherwise they'll be flooded by people commenting that the same has occurred to them.

If a company replies in a bad way, acting like an inexperienced shop clerk, the pillory ignites.

One evening I bought a carton of milk at my local supermarket. The next morning I opened it and realized it had gone sour.

IF BUSINESSES WANT TO BE ON SOCIAL NETWORKS AND HAVE THEIR SAY, THEY SHOULD ENCOURAGE CONVERSATIONS, CONFRONTATIONS AND DISCUSSIONS

The problem, though, was that it had not expired: most probably someone had left it out of the refrigerated aisle. I went back to the supermarket and told the salesgirl what had happened. She replied that 'such things happen, because as soon as you take a product out of the supermarket, it goes sour because of the variation in temperature'. I burst into a laughter and promised the following morning I would bring my cereals from home to have breakfast with her. She apologized and handed me a replacement milk carton.

I immediately envisioned what would have happened if she had given that reply on Facebook on behalf of her company. Somebody would have probably grabbed a screenshot and posted it on a Facebook page or group, one such as 'Epic fails'; here it would have spread across a multitude of comedy and irony communities, and then among the populist groups with all their anti-multinational slogans, and eventually journalists would have picked it for a gallery on the 'Huffington Post' or the front page of an online newspaper. The bottom line: a viral case, a company crisis, managers forced to apologize. Hell breaking loose for a milk carton.

This was an exceptional case – or maybe not, according to some recent events –, but try and visit the Facebook page of a basic service provider, such as a phone company, and have a look at the comments under each post. You'll probably see a post about the Venice Film Festival, with user Saul politely commenting: 'Good evening, last night my Internet connection stopped working. Can you please fix it?'. Then you'll find Anna's more genuine and slightly ungrammatical remark: 'Think of me instead! The Waifi is borken. What happens? I writed to your site and nobody answer me'.

It happens every time: a company may hire the best creatives in advertisement history, have them conceive the year's best campaign and even win some awards, but there will always be a commenter paying no attention to a post's contents and use it to complain about some inefficiency.

So, what does having a social account or page really mean? It means owning a communication channel, that users will use to reach out to your company. Companies must learn to do two things: they must come up with interesting and useful things to tell their customers and they must be ready to wittily reply to what customers tell them.

And yet so many businesses still believe the smartest choice is a one-directional conversation, something along the lines of: 'Hello, we're Company X and have no interest in understanding your opinion on Facebook; we just need you to 'Like' our page and maybe listen to us when we post our contents and our offers'. Well, now picture me at the supermarket, now dealing with a saleswoman who, after looking at my sour milk carton, simply turns her back and goes away, without saying a word, or tries to sell me biscuits.

A good CRM is a vital part of online communication and cannot be improvised. As a matter of fact, it must be set up before even going social. Companies can't do without it because if they're caught off guard they'll lose their customer base. What bothers me is why companies attend media training classes and crisis management lessons for their offline activities but don't do the same for their online presence.

Performing some good CRM means preparing every possible

question in advance along with a proactive reply, one that doesn't sparkle other issues – justifications often trigger further complaints – and displays a level of kindness that won't make the customer angry but burns off any controversy instead.

In general, companies ought to always handle the following macro-categories of interactions: complaints about their products, complaints about their service, complaints about operator's mistakes at and outside their stores, and requests for information.

Good answers aren't enough, though. If I post my problem and I'm simply told it will be handled, I'm not satisfied. It gets me even angrier when I'm asked to call another number, because most of the times it is the number I have already called and that has kept me on hold for hours. Things don't get any better when I'm told: 'We'll check and let you know'. In such cases, a week later nobody has reached back to me, not even to ask me how I am.

A standardized flow between social CRM and internal departments must be in place in every company, because I want my problem to be solved *now*, not *one day*, God only knows when.

And I want this to happen in any case, whether I call an operator, I visit a store or post a complaint on Facebook.

I don't really care about what the company's internal procedures are or

118

if they prefer to be contacted via phone or other channels. I'm the one who picks the channel. I'm the one who knows whether I'm satisfied.

3.3 CHATBOTS

Not so long ago, Sina Bank implemented a Web bot that quickly replies to users requesting information about general services and bank accounts. A user willing to know how much his wife has spent in clothes in the past week can ask so via chat and gets an instant reply. Things like chatbots are now everywhere and we're all studying them. Facebook keeps on introducing updated *releases* of its codes so that chatbots can be programmed on Messenger. The reason is simple: if Facebook attracts a company to his platform to discuss with their customers, the people at Facebook will know everything about both the customers and the company, and customers will most probably buy their services, because going anywhere else won't be convenient anymore. When I told some friends about this, they replied: 'Why should I use a chat that instantly replies when I already have a home banking service, which is safer and allows me to perform all operations?'. That's the same answer I got from some upper-level managers. I already have something that does everything, why should I need another system?

The digital business never allows for shortcuts or simplifications.

People want to save time and chatbots are the next frontier when it comes to saving time on social networks. No calculations involved, no middle steps, no need to wait for the system to boot. Just one click, one question, the occasional voice message and what we need appears right on our screen.

To achieve this, a company needs:

1) a good database;
2) a serious CRM analysis, blended with SEO.

First of all, if you're a company you need to know very well what your customers ask for. Selecting all the questions they submit to your call center is not enough. Sometimes they just browse your website and look for answers to questions they won't ask to a living person. And this happens because they're ashamed, or they haven't thought about asking, or for any other reason. That's why browsing flows are crucial. Not the most common, which are easy to find, though. We're talking about *all* browsing flows, because 'less common' users don't have a lesser value than others. As a matter of fact, sometimes they're the ones who turn into bigger spending customers.

Here's an easy scenario: I've never contacted my bank's call center but a bot would surely suit me. But will such bot be able to also perform all the steps I usually take on my own? I know that bots won't be able to do everything at first, but if I get accustomed to having an on-the-fly reply about the amount that's sitting in my account, a year later I may be ready to get the details about stock shares via a simple request. I know I'll still need to authorize the bond purchase, but also I expect an ultra-fast development of this technology to take place. I'm ready to let it become a habit for me, but it'll have to come meet me halfway.

Flows are not enough: you need to understand what people ask. Some early help may come from your SEO and semantic analyses, before you move to artificial intelligence.

If your engineers monitor everything people look up about your products on search engines, they'll end up finding other potential questions you might be asked. Those who settle for the most searched keywords or website rankings need to learn that Google is a true goldmine for information and ideas, good for improving both their product positioning and products themselves.

On online forums – yes, they still survive and actually thrive, get over it – your customers discuss how they can resume their smartphones after an OS upgrade or why a device can't read memory cards anymore. These are the things people look for in forums because call center operators either don't have the faintest idea of what callers are talking about or aren't skilled enough for overtly technical questions that need some background training – training is a cost for companies and many don't want to invest – or are so overburdened that they cannot promptly take calls.

A chatbot that can easily answer all questions, including the most technical, even by simply showing a relevant tutorial, would be a huge leap forward and would provide a remarkable service.

A bot needs to connect to a database, so that it can both retrieve and input information. For some topics this would be an easy and intuitive task. A user requesting an account balance needs it right away with no unneeded waiting. The system must query the database, fetch what the user asks for and display it on the screen. That's it.

There's a further potential, though, which is something a good call center usually can provide: the retrieval of my 'position' and records, everything I own and do, everything I need and would like to do. By reading what I most frequently ask, a bot can anticipate me or detect a potential issue and either solve it or escalate it to a more skilled operator.

A chatbot-database exchange is much more than a website mechanism, it's an essential step for logging everything a user asks a chatbot.

Once information is stored in the database, analysts have enough data to either learn what customers search in general or divide them into small targets and assess every single individual's requirements. This allows a company to identify every little need from its different audiences and improve their service accordingly.

A properly configured chatbot is the Industry 4.0 of CRM.

Just as in Industry 4.0 companies can analyze all manufacturing steps and the operation of their products using sensors in order to prevent waste, errors and malfunctioning, now they can do the same for their customer relationships.

The abilities to record anything and the technology to do it are all in place. If a company is good enough, such triggers can lead to a great improvement in their products.

There's a final topic we should cover, and it's artificial intelligence, or AI.

If a bot doesn't automatically learn, then it's useless.

There's no actual improvement if a company simply allocates dozens of experts who prepare every single pair of possible answers and questions that users will need to type word for word (otherwise the system asks them to 'Try again').

Customers are not dumb, most of the times they're tired and don't want to waste their time. If a company does so, customers get angry and go somewhere else. People are frustrated by their smartphone's voice interface never getting their questions right, thus feeding rambling replies. A customer's patience should never be abused. Artificial intelligence must ensure that, after one mistake, the bot immediately understands what a customer is asking and improves the answer.

A professional chat should never be less smart than Akinator, the online game by French company elokence.com featuring a genie guessing a famous character after asking the user some questions. Akinator was very popular around 2015-2016 because it successfully showcased one of the qualities of connecting technology to communication: the ability to learn.

I only recently tried it again and I must say it's really improved a lot. I decided to challenge it and thought about Mario Faccenda, who played football with Fiorentina back in the Nineties, and the system got it. This means that either somebody before me had typed this specific footballer's name or Akinator plumbed the whole Web and recorded everything. So I tried with a more obscure footballer, Marco Marchi. Akinator did not find him right away but, since it was in one of its databases, his name was eventually returned.

I'm totally serious when I say that my chat has lesser logging skills than Akinator and this actually poses a problem.

3.4 WHAT'S NEXT?

Some say Facebook is an operating system, but its user experience is actually moving towards augmented-reality entertainment, from videogames to art, from tourism to porn.

Mr. Zuckerberg got it first and invested on it, as numbers seem to suggest. He announced that by 2020 there'll be 5 million Oculus Rifts in the world. Maybe they'll be a prerogative of the riches or the hyper-geeks, but they'll mark the beginning of a new revolution. If everything is becoming 3D and virtual/augmented reality, digital technology will act as the interface we'll use to steer this revolution. And social networks will be the tool we'll rely on when enjoying this new form of entertainment.

Today, social networks are experiencing an involution and they're becoming increasingly boring every day. A lovely tool we used to stay in touch with our friends has turned into a huge, ongoing press review with an endless set of tricks and gimmicks to get more 'Likes' and collect as much information on people as possible. Once there were only newspapers, then came the new media, now we have a plethora of fake accounts and pages filled with yada-yada and unverified news.

This is 'the Zuckerberg way': to provide increasingly less in general, while giving increasingly more to a single user. This is achieved by always saying the same things and by wondering how a brand can attract an average user.

Many believe that if you don't do it right away, and be a pioneer in your market, you'll never succeed. I believe this to be too pessimistic, but it's undoubtedly hard to attract somebody's attention when you're out of their *filter bubble*. That's what Facebook ads were introduced for. Companies are paying in order to reach back the audience that had originally 'Liked' them. It may seem a win-win strategy, but the only winner here is in fact Mark Zuckerberg.

So what will become of social networks? Small businesses will probably find it increasingly harder to stay relevant, since users will only look for the things they're interested in. If *filter bubbles* are further shrunk, so that the average Facebook user only finds alike-thinking friends and cat lovers groups, a company will struggle to penetrate, participate in discussions or show users that other opportunities and discussion topics exist out there. Our interests aren't broadening, but narrowing. The problem is that companies *need* to be on social networks and this makes things difficult. CRM is a good way to get in, but social networks are currently migrating towards 'experiences', and that's why

Zuckerberg has purchased Oculus, an application that can allow brands to really thrive. Users make experiences via either huge screen or social networks, and not incidentally in a few year the latter will coincide with the former. Our homes are going to experience the same revolution that occurred in our pockets: we'll have a screen the size we want, most probably equipped with a voice interface, and it will be either a computer or a TV according to our needs.

Businesses will probably sponsor our experiences, or help us enjoy them. Recently, Italian fashion brand Nero Giardini offered their fans outfit suggestions via Facebook.

Subscribed users are tagged in a picture showing the brand's latest collection. What Nero Giardini does with images today may be done with virtual reality tomorrow.

TODAY, SOCIAL NETWORKS ARE EXPERIENCING AN INVOLUTION AND THEY ARE BECOMING INCREASINGLY BORING EVERY DAY

A company that doesn't simply suggest some 3D outfit pairings but allows users to try them out: this is the ultimate experience.

Many other examples are already in place. YouTube is packed with 3D visits of buildings such as London's Westminster, though the resolution is still not high enough. Or you can step inside the Lego factory and see how the Lego bricks are made, or join a live concert held at the Maldives, or scuba dive at the Coral Reef.

It's still a simple 3D effect created by a 360° camera and, though it looks great on Google Cardboards, it doesn't allow much freedom of movement: the user can only move along with the camera, turn around or look any direction. However, this technology may allow two friends who live in two different cities – say, Milan and San Francisco – to catch up using their Oculus devices and visit each other's house, greet their families and pets and even enjoy the view from each other's windows. But this is just a fraction of what Facebook can do; companies hold the biggest share and have some huge opportunities. Their media budget must include a production budget. The experience must and will be of the highest quality. Sure, you pay for quality. But quality pays off.

I dream one day I'll be able to try out a trip before I take it. I don't simply want to look at some pictures or videos, I want to enjoy the actual 3D experience, like in a videogame. And what about sports? Live broadcasts may include a small control room to switch across cameras, including a 360° or 3D camera allowing me to follow the gameplay from the field. Or it could be a basketball dunk as seen from the hoop, a speeding Ferrari from the pilot's helmet showing me what you see when you drive at 180 mph.

And what about the news? Recently, Smart News Agency sent a journalist with six camera mounted on his head to Jisr al-Shughur, Syria, a few kilometers from the Turkish border, to report on the town's ghost districts during the war. In the video the reporter doesn't speak much and if he does he only explains where he is and what has happened. The rest is done by images, using an angle that shows everything around the man. The effect is striking, because we may have grown accustomed to war photography and pictures of suffering children, but here you have the chance to actually walk inside a building, and all you see is rubble. It gives you a sense of utter desolation and anguish, with not a single teardrop shown on screen. Our own tears are enough.

The future of social networking is 3D infotainment, made with videos and drones. Cameras will be mounted on drones, installed inside their electric eyes. We'll be able to remote-fly them across the world, we'll take panning shots on the beach just like we used to do with our webcams: soon we'll be moving a drone around the planet and watch people enjoy their mojitos at a seaside kiosk in Zanzibar. A drone or a robot will travel in our place and make us have some fun.

But drones won't only be good to take future-generation selfies. The next Formula 1 or Moto GP races will be drone races. Drones instead of cars, bikes or dogs. And I'll be the one who controls a racing drone, from home. I'll sit comfortably on my couch and, after turning on the app, I'll be on a race circuit in Dubai. I'll wear my 3D visor and look at my opponents: other drones. And then ready, set... go! I'll be twitching, driving my speeding drone at 180 mph amongst the lights. My friends will be following my race from their social channels, using their reactions to cheer, and I'll see their 'Likes' scrolling in my visor, along with the names of those who are betting real money on me via their smartphones. Viewers will switch from one reality to another, from a racer to another. They will get inside my drone's eyes with me. As a matter of fact, my reality will be extended in a much wider and immersive way than a pair of Google glasses can do now. The drones will be actually racing and I'll feel like I'm flying at 180 mph, but they may do pretty anything in my place. For better or worse, this potential exists: it'll allow me to shop for groceries without leaving my house but also to check that strange crackle outside my window or to visit an archeological site. My drone will walk on my behalf, as I discover the treasures of Pompeii. This will probably make some people very lazy, but also convince others to go and enjoy the real thing. And book a flight to Naples right away.

Chapter 4
A NEW STORYTELLING

4.1 IS CONTENT **KING?**

In *The Founder,* the movie about the man who made the McDonald's empire back in the Seventies, a very cunning finance manager explains that the actual gain of the McDonald's chain comes from renting out thousands of franchisees across the USA, not from selling hamburgers.

Every day, marketers like us ask ourselves what business we're in, and what businesses our clients are in. Let me say this provocatively: all of us are in the 'reassurance business'.

Advertisers reassure media strategists that a message is right. Media strategists reassure brand managers that the proper target audience is being addressed. Brand managers reassure CEOs that all the above steps ensure our products have the visibility and *equity* to hit the right people, who love us in return and will always say good things about us.

But common people aren't in any business. They have behaviors, that constantly change; they evolve or involve according to the moment in history, our economic conditions, social phenomena and our way of life.

Just a few years ago we could have never imagined that a 5-inch screen would become an ever-present filter between us and the rest of the world while we're on an underground train or wait for the bus, while we watch TV or have dinner with our girlfriend, and even while we're driving or lie in bed before we fall asleep.

We're constantly distracted by something and entertained by something else. So, though it's hard to admit it, we're in the 'distraction business'. People are hungry for contents, contents of any type (images, texts, videos), contents no matter what, contents we can maul and digest so that we can make room for even more contents.

We're in the distraction business and contents are our asset and a safe haven, just as gold coins were for our grandparents.

Hordes of quasi-journalists, quasi-writers, quasi-poets fill pages and screens with almost anything. The most cunning of them simply copy and paste contents and adapt or translate bits and pieces that were drifting in the Internet ocean. And then there's us: the mapmakers.

Here's a hint about the volume of user-generated data: at any given minute, and on Facebook alone, 510 comments are posted, 293,000 new statuses are updated and 136,000 pictures are uploaded.[7] This means that, as a high number of active and engagement-oriented users are actually on the platform, a huge mass of contents are fighting to get these users' attention: strategies and quality are crucial, or at least what readers perceive (and not necessarily what we mean) as such. In May 2013, 4.75 billion contents were shared daily on Facebook, marking a 94% increase from August 2012.[8]

According to a report by Gwawa[9] based on official figures released by different social networks, from 2013 to the present day the number of Twitter posts has increased by 25% and reached 350,000 posts per minute. **YouTube figures more than tripled in the last two years, with 400 hours of video uploaded every minute.** In the same timeframe, Instagram users clicked the heart icon under 2.5 million pictures. The amount of Facebook posts has increased by 22% since 2013, going from 2.5 to 3 million posts per minute. This marks a 300% increase from 2011, when post were 650,000 per minute.

Facebook users 'Like' more than 4 million posts every 60 seconds, which equals to about 6 billion posts clicked every day. Every hour, 4

[7] Source: thesocialskinny.com
[8] Source: Facebook.
[9] Source: https://www.gwava.com/blog/internet-data-created-daily.

million searches are performed on Google, while 4 million instant messages are sent in the USA alone. It's a huge mass of data being uploaded every day. A day is made of 1,440 minutes, so on any given day 500 million tweets are sent, more than 4 million hours of video are uploaded to YouTube, 3.6 billion Instagram pictures get a heart, 4.3 billion Facebook posts are published and the 'Like' button is clicked 5.75 billion times, 40 million tweets are shared and 6 billion searches are made on Google.

This increase in social media use doesn't imply a reduction in emails: in 2015, 205 billion messages[10] were sent, while a 20% increase (246 billion emails) is expected in 2019.

Firms, newspapers, companies are as active as common people.

When we open the faucet of our databases, we generate a flow, a stream, a path. Do we want urban young males to read about sports? It's done. Do we want elder housewives to get in touch with the Web by means of gossip? No problem. And so on and on, until late in the evening, and through the night.

And the morning after, with more targets, pieces, maps. There's a huge

[10] Source: Radicati Group http://www.radicati.com/wp/wp-content/uploads/2015/02/Email-Statistics- Report-2015-2019-Executive-Summary.pdf.

hunger for contents, to generate them is one of the jobs of the future. In a decade or two, an increasing number of articles and news will be tailored around me, videos will talk directly to me, as they will be dynamically generated by a matrix of millions of possible combinations. A huge workload for actors, voice talents, video editors, illustrators, directors. Most probably, almost everything will be of very low quality, just enough to quickly entertain, engage, distract us. **People find their own distraction, then follow and cuddle it: an article, a video, a cartoon. They comment, share, generate discussions.** If you ask anybody how much time they spend online with social networks, news, search engines, you always get the same reply: 'Not much, just a few minutes'. The truth is that 39 million Italians surf the Internet for about 6 hours a day from a computer and 2 hours from a mobile phone.[11] And it is quite a lot.

Most people don't even realize.

IN ABOUT A DECADE I'LL FIND MORE AND MORE ARTICLES TAILORED AROUND ME, GENERATED BY A MATRIX OF MILLIONS OF POSSIBLE COMBINATIONS

---

[11] Source: We Are Social – Digital 2017: http://wearesocial.com/it/blog/2017/01/digital-in-2017-in-italia-e-nel-mondo

Sometimes those who generate these flows place some little obstacles on our way, like data to submit or actions to perform.

We just click 'here', and 'Like' something and then move on, and this feeds the databases and fine-tunes their knowledge about us.

According to American writer Terence McKenna 'the engineers of the future will be poets'. Paraphrasing his adage, we may say that **storytelling is a story that can elicit emotions, explain the why's, illustrate the how's and encourage a listener to look for the what's.** Storytelling holds emotions that are more connected to a product or company's story rather than facts; it uses our senses to describe a product; it centers around the 'why'. Moreover, it creates a brand new world or conception of a product or company in the listener's mind, not based on a set of immaterial features that are inherent to the product or service; it doesn't aim at convincing but at involving; it triggers lateral thinking. As the Hopi American Indian tribe say: 'Those who tell the stories, rule the world'.

Storytelling belongs to advertising because, till recently, companies used to promote a product by showing it in a 30-second TV break that was watched by millions of people. Those millions still exist but don't watch television anymore, or maybe we're finally admitting that they probably weren't watching even back then.

At the end of the day, even when I'm in front of my TV, I have my mobile phone in my hand and I basically mind my own business.

Television has become some sort of background noise to me. We used to consider our mobile phones, smartphones and tablets as our *second*

'THE ENGINEERS OF THE FUTURE WILL BE POETS'

_Terence McKenna

screens. Now things have totally reversed: now our television has undoubtedly become our second screen, since the *first screen* is the one we have in front of us, the one we really care about.

The way TV series are being currently made proves this point: action scenes, mostly car chasing and shooting scenes, are usually placed at standstills across a storyline, their noise aimed at distracting viewers from their mobile phones as they tweet or chat while 'watching' TV. It's all because we have stopped paying attention.

If we're scrolling through our Facebook wall on our smartphone and somebody talks to us, we're not really listening. This is the brutal truth, period. Scientifically and technically speaking, we can't do both things simultaneously.

The first thing we should be aware of is that platforms have changed. A screen that is so close to our eyes outdoes all other screens and events, which are literally pushed to the background.

The second thing is that, ironically, we've found out that the future of our ability of engaging people actually comes from the past: *Carosello.*[12]

Each short film featured in *Carosello* would tell a story, it was eight, ten, even fifteen minute long and only displayed the advertised product at the end. It was a nice and funny way for a brand to put their signature under a tale that had just been told and that didn't necessarily share a connection to the product. Then advertisers like us came by, and brought along their market researches, their focus groups, the idea that people were intrigued by our messages and in no time 5,000 messages started to flood in, 5,000 messages a day, and we all succumbed to them. They're too many, and people get distracted or have learned how not to acknowledge them. At best, people are not paying attention and advertisers don't know how to push their commercial messages through to them. **So now we're revamping the *Carosello* model from the Sixties, sell it as a breakthrough because we call it by a new name: 'storytelling'.**

---

[12] 'Carosello (Italian for 'carousel') was an Italian television advertising show, broadcast on RAI from 1957 to 1977. The series mainly showed short sketch comedy films using live action, animation, and puppetry.' (Source: Wikipedia)

Very few brands can afford telling a story.

Think about *lovemarks*. The concept comes from Kevin Roberts of Saatchi&Saatchi Australia, and is quite simple: if you own an iPhone and you break it, you'll most probably buy another iPhone, because Apple is much more than a company to you, it's a brand you actually love, a *lovemark*.

Aldo always has lunch with a can of Coke Zero Sugar and if you take it away from him, he gets angry. Coke Zero Sugar is a *lovemark* to him. It's also

WE'VE FOUND OUT THAT THE FUTURE OF OUR ABILITY OF ENGAGING PEOPLE ACTUALLY COMES FROM THE PAST: CAROSELLO

a *useful mark*, because he likes it and it makes him feel good. Some time ago, I decided to migrate to Apple products: iPhone and iPad. Well, I'd never buy Android devices now. I don't like them, I don't find them user-friendly or 'me-friendly'. It is a matter of efficiency, also. When my Fitbit broke up I bought it back again, and that's why it is a *lovemark* to me. A child's *lovemark* may be Pringles. Even water can be a *lovemark*: some people only buy Voss water bottles.

I have nothing against *lovemarks*.

I simply believe that **many brands can't afford to be *lovemarks*, yet they need to exist and tell a story nonetheless. The problem is that, pretty often, their story is not interesting at all.**

One thing we know is that brands were made to make products more easily recognizable, and that there are dozens of products that we don't know about because they simply are pieces of other products.

Take lamps, for instance: not everyone has Artemide as their *lovemark*. We don't usually choose a company that makes a single piece of aluminum or another small component as our *lovemark*. We usually only have a partial view of a product: we love Ferrari or another automotive brand, but there are thousands of components inside a car that are manufactured by companies that we've never heard about. One interesting case is Brembo, the brake manufacturing company that was great in transforming something for which most of us don't care at all into an element of recognizability. They turned brakes into something that's as recognizable as a shining branded muffler on a hotrod. A great idea.

I believe that all brands want to – or *think* they can – tell a story,

but most people are not interested in such stories.

Truthfully, I don't know if I'm interested in the story of my bank , but it may be the bank's own fault. American banks always tell their story. Take Wells Fargo and its logo: a classic stage coach driven by six horses. Wells Fargo used to be a logistics company, freighting goods from one place to another, just like in the Old Wild West. Not only goods, as a matter of fact, but money as well. This is how Wells Fargo was born in California and that's why the stage coach is still featured everywhere. They treasure and update their own tradition, sometimes even to the extremes. On the more refined Italian market scenario, the stagecoach, even in its original layout with colorful horses, is a clash for your eyes.

What the people at Wells Fargo do is trying to keep their history alive in the digital arena and in our completely different world. It's Italians who did it all wrong. We had some historic banks, such as Monte dei Paschi di Siena, dating back to the 15th Century. Or Credito Italiano, known as the 'bank in a double-breasted suit', because of a very successful TV ad that used to air back in the days and featured a woman – I still remember her – wearing a double-breasted suit, a symbol for elegance, gravitas and so on.

We actually tarnished our brands. Obviously, some bank groups have nothing to say about themselves, because they're the result of mergers. They were born just a couple of days ago and they lost their history along the way. You will never hear them say: 'I come from the merger of *n* banks'. They simply pick the one brand that is perceived as the best or has a century-old presence in Italian history and keep it.

Apparently, Italian companies don't want to respect their brands, or they're incapable of doing so.

Barclays may acquire fifty different banks, but it will never change, because it has a high and strong respect for its own brand. Similarly, we would never rename Generali – one of the major insurance companies in the world, right up there with Allianz or Fidelity – into something like 'Digital Gen'.

Generali has an important story to tell and could never change its name. If it did so, it would discard the strength of a brand which is a part of our culture and has had a major role in our contemporary history.

Digital platforms, a constellation where people usually complain about things that aren't working, are surely pushing us to create a new form of storytelling. People are hungry for contents and novelties.

While some brands have based their storytelling on their past, others try to look ahead and have become synonyms for 'the future'.

I strongly doubt that Apple will ever start claiming they invented the first Macintosh computer in 1982, because they have surpassed that product a million times already and they still keep on surpassing it every six months with their keynote events.

Monte dei Paschi may get better results by working on traditions, because future banks will be very different from today's banks. **Somehow, storytelling reveals what brands and products will become.** Here is an example. If I said: 'In ten years we'll have an Apple Bank', you could close your eyes and picture it: all white, with its own credit card, an Apple Bank with money and liquidity. An Apple Store alone has the actual liquidity to act as a bank (by opening lines of credit, and so on). Speaking of *lovemarks*, if Apple had a bank, how many of us would open an account there?

Can you imagine a Starbucks Bank as well? Inventing a possible future for some businesses can be an intriguing game. An Apple Bank is the result of the amount of cash spent at Apple Stores. Storytelling can also foretell a possible future. Among the things I believe in are user-generated contents. I like it when a brand tells his own story. But I still haven't realized, or maybe I still can't see, what the meaning and effectiveness of a brand's storytelling as told by its customers can be. The examples are still very few.

Telling the story of a brand is something that every business has done and that can be experienced in many different ways.

I remember an ad by AT&T (digital media, not shown on TV) showing a black mother asking a man why he had texted while driving on that day, thus killing her son in the resulting car crash.

Though this was a social awareness campaign, AT&T was also saying something about their brand, positioning it in terms of its values despite the risk of linking it to a hard topic such as death. No brand would have done that in Italy. Italian telecom providers would never have the guts to say that something bad can happen while using their services or products. AT&T was incredibly strong in saying: 'We're giving you the best service, but please try and use it responsibly. You cannot take somebody's life'.

I don't think storytelling can necessarily be based on a customer's statement. **Via digital technologies, consumers say something about a product or service every day**; their act of purchasing, their satisfaction, their disappointment. Customers give their commentaries every day. Many Italian companies do not really embrace this ongoing narration, they just let it flow without even watching into it, verifying it or improving themselves and their business. They don't take any advantage of this huge agent of continuous feedback.

4.2 MY OWN **ADVERTISEMENT**

Our browsers store all of our behaviors, even if our real life is hopefully larger and more impenetrable than a simple cache memory. The evolution of communication messages and our ability to target them to dedicated audiences go hand in hand with technology. It's not about some new amazing breakthroughs, it's about learning about our behaviors by using simple software technologies and collecting information from our actions. Once they have tracked down something interesting, these programs act almost immediately or accumulate more data to define their forms of action.

Our Web activities yield 2.5 quintillion (2.5 followed by 17 zeroes) bytes of data every day. This amount of files could be stored on ten million Blu-ray disks: pile them up and you'll get four Eiffel towers on top of each other. 90% of data available today were generated in the past two years. This amazingly huge amount of information can be logged by our browsers and, partly, by the Websites we visit.[13]

---

[13] Source: http://www.vcloudnews.com/every-day-big-data-statistics-2-5-quintillion-bytes-of-data-created-daily/

Once a user receives a 'cookie' (a file that stores a user's online activities to be later read and monitored by websites), the variable of incoming requests and information allows us to immediately learn who a user is according to their reference sector.

Digital managers stand at the end of this timeline waiting, because that's when a consumer will start looking for a specific product. Or they try and classify them according to the products they purchase and the websites they visit.

I believe we don't actually realize how things have changed and progressed. Think of what happens the moment you land on a Web page and how your actions that are traced on that page can be used for other purposes. Digital contents are undergoing a major two-fold branching that Italy is starting to experience only now, but Americans have been mastering it for some time: content recommendation and marketing automation.

Via algorithms, bigger server capacities and a huge set of available tools companies can now learn a single individual's digital behavior.

If they wanted to, they could narrow their target audience to 35-year-old females living in the Bovisa district of Milan and supporting Inter, one of the local football teams.

Information can be increasingly targeted and made *one-to-one*. Content recommendation is the 'cognitive' ability of algorithms to process information and actually learn who the people in the extremely accurate target I have defined are, in order to provide the most suitable contents to each user.

An amazing, game-changing fact is that if you land on any of today's online catalogs, from an e-commerce portal to a video streaming website, the amount

TODAY WE CAN LEARN A SINGLE INDIVIDUAL'S DIGITAL BEHAVIOUR

of contents you'll find is so overwhelming that you'll psychologically tend to rule it out. When too much stuff is available, humans are prone to think that there's nothing really suitable for them.

Instead, if cognitive systems are built and users only accurate and suitable contents, companies will get two different benefits: they'll increase their sales ability and they'll make a user believe that their catalog is endless.

Netflix has made content recommendation its biggest strength.

If you compare its movies to any other pay TV's catalog, Netflix's offer is much inferior but an average user won't really mind or notice. Netflix's strength is its ability to exactly understand a user's profile, and profiling starts at registration when a user provides a number of initial information. Later, users will display a selection of suitable contents and, at their next login, Netflix's powerful content recommendation system will only feed them with the most compatible titles. This process has nothing to do with the old method of showing a catalog 'as it is', the same contents being displayed to all users in a single 1,000 film list, the system being unable to remember a user's previous choices at login. When users have to start all over again, they eventually stop using a streaming service.

This is what Apple TV and iTunes do: they display the same contents to all users. They highlight the new releases, the most popular choices, but don't use very sophisticated algorithms.

However, very evolved content recommendation algorithms exist and are just about to spread across multimedia and catalog contents. Until recently, it was technically impossible to do some true *one-to-one* marketing because of the limitations of available tools. Sill today, however, if companies want to create digital contents they need a database to extract data from and the more variables are cross-checked, the longer the processing takes. Systems take hours to *query* a database about who a user is, where he's from, what he's doing and so on... But companies can't afford to waste their customers' time by asking them to wait while matches are found. When this happens, users eventually lose their patience and never come back.

Cognitive algorithms can now get to a *one-to-one* level that was unthinkable in the past. Clustering users into groups was the best companies could achieve. They'd go: 'Considering a number of variables, I can offer this sweater to all blond males who own this hat'. It only involved some database processing. New algorithms can put together a huge pieces of information in a few milliseconds and single out the closest product to a consumer's purchasing habits. This true *one-to-one* marketing opportunity is a major breakthrough for digital businesses.

Recently, Google tested a set of advertising billboards and I can predict their possible future applications.

Using data collected from my online searches, my emails, my favorite videos on YouTube, Google knows me better than I think.

After voice-activating my destination in my environment-friendly self-driving car's navigation device, I'll sink into my comfortable backseat couch.

Here I'll wear my augmented-reality VR glasses to watch an episode of my favorite TV series, I'll stay up-to-date with the latest news or I'll simply look out the window. All of these actions I'll probably do at the same time.

While enjoying the landscape I'll realize that a new advertising billboard has been installed at a highway junction.

The displayed messages will strike me: it'll seem that they were (and they were, actually) custom made for me. I'll watch the ad for my favorite band's upcoming gig, the tickets for which I'll have looked up that very morning; and then I'll see the image of extra soft toilet paper I was going to buy on my way back. I'll also find an ad for my favorite shoes. (What a coincidence! My old pair had just worn out!) I'll be the only one to see all these products, as they're exclusive to me, suitably displayed to satisfy my preferences and needs. If I want, I will be able to purchase them right away and they'll be shipped to my home in an hour: all I'll have to do is blink at what I want to purchase.

Once back home, I'll take off my VR glasses and rub my eyes. And I'll wonder: what if I have never left my sofa in my living room? What if all my experiences throughout my day were only virtual?

It would be unbelievable, yet not impossible.

My thoughts will be interrupted by the door bell. I'll go to the door and a drone will have dropped a package on my doormat. I'll open it and find a supply of ultra-soft toilet paper inside.

Just what I need.

4.3 A BILLION **AUTOMATIC CUSTOM DISCOUNTS**

A turning point also lies in communication, because communication happens when a customer steps into a store as well.

Just picture a last-generation retail store. Customers' mobile phones have an app installed, collecting their loyalty card points. Algorithms allow the company to review the customers' actual purchases and buying habits so they can send them – as soon as they're past the store door – some dedicated, ad hoc *push notifications*.

If companies know the habits of every single customer, they can feed *one-to-one promotions* based on each individual's purchases and needs. They can either display two items that are close to a customer's beloved product or show them their beloved product straight away. They can create a customized shopping list that doesn't exceed a customer's average budget but also benefits the company's own margin.

Generic promotions and offers can be bypassed if a company directly tells a yogurt enthusiast to buy a product because she (and nobody else) is entitled to a special 15% discount. This way, the customer is satisfied and the company can apply a *one-to-one* discount via a clearly defined marketing action.

All of this has an impact 'marketing automation', which works by inserting 'triggers', signals that associate specific behaviors to specific actions.

Marketing works on predictions, as it accurately monitors and analyzes a customer's behavior.

Alerts and notifications can be either responsive and proactive, and enforce specific actions accordingly.

Things don't need to be planned when they happen, as they're planned in advance through automated behaviors.

We're still a long way from understanding how important targetization and target-based differences are in communication.

In a Content Marketing Institute research about North American benchmarks, budgets and trends in 2017, a number of content marketers whose current performances were better than in 2016 were asked what factors they thought were responsible for their organization's improvement within the scope of their global success. Among the answers, content distribution (more targeted contents, singling out of successful actions) was only reported by 50% of respondents, while a high emphasis was still attributed to creativity and real time marketing.[14] In other words, companies' efforts are still more focused on reacting to events in real time, just like Ceres's ironic instant campaigns in Italy, than developing their own strategy.

The world of communication and creativity has a twofold path ahead: on one hand, the evolution of marketing departments made of people who are more and more experienced in digital technologies and figures, along with interaction dashboards and analysis groups with an increasingly planned, scientific, almost army-like approach; on the other hand, the development of a 'high end' line of storytelling – because communication cannot be separated from creativity – applied to short viral videos, direct marketing actions or

IF YOU KNOW EVERY SINGLE CUSTOMER'S HABITS YOU CAN MAKE ONE-TO-ONE PROMOTIONS

---

[14]Source: http://contentmarketinginstitute.com/wp-content/uploads/2016/11/2017_B2B_Research_ FINAL-11-2-16.pdf

huge branding campaigns, all of which will be increasingly tied to telling a story. Kickstarter is a good example: every campaign on its platform is complemented with some emotional videos telling a modern-day fable and conveying the campaigners' enthusiasm and commitment. It is of little relevance that, as it often occurs, many of their revolutionary products eventually fail.

The revolution will happen within organizations. A company's feet must be firmly on both grounds: **a business needs to use both analog and digital tools and to enlist constantly-evolving professionals who understand each other and know about almost everything.**

This is the core of a successful corporate strategy.

4.4 A DIFFERENT STORYTELLING **FOR EACH CUSTOMER**

The overwhelming presence of contents requires the use of storytelling, which in fact originated in this era of rapidly-ageing things. In the past, broadcasting a TV commercial two weeks a year was good enough; today, TV ads (and the digital contents that support and supplement them, and which are shorter and need to be continuously fed to the audience) must be on the point.

Some say the frequency of TV ads will be further decreased. But online contents – their need to be ongoing and spread across all devices (smartphones, tablets, PCs, and so on) posing a risk of audience annoyance – will need to be strictly moderated: their message can be penalized if users grow tired of them.

In storytelling, contents must be continuously renewed, otherwise they'll be frustrated by multi-device vision.

That's why brands need to tell and tell themselves some sort of stories with a silver thread through campaigns with meaningful and related contents. This requires an attention to contents that was didn't exist

159

before: if you sell clothes, you can obviously make a website with product pictures featuring colors, sizes, shapes, patterns, and so on. But a garment performs much better if it is shown within a storyline, and worn by someone: it evolves from an amorphous object shown on a white page to a contextualized item that is consistent with the company's brand identity, the story of its manufacturing process, the source of its materials. In other words, it must be fascinating for readers/viewers.

In the past, there used to be lots of monthly and weekly magazines, biannual mail catalogues (such as 'Postalmarket' in Italy), and companies had all the time they needed to make them. In turn, TV advertisement suffered huge pressures because of the time needed to conceive, film, edit a commercial and buy the advertising spaces. With digital technology, a product must be dipped into real life and comply to the brand's essence. There are no time constraints when you show your contents, thus you can prevent users from being discouraged by possible excesses.

The aforementioned *Carosello* was the beginning of this, because to its storytelling nature, as were the early 20th Century posters by Campari or Fiat that featured hand drawings (by masters such as Depero and

Sironi) because black and white pictures were not appealing. If they still existed today, we'd have 365 different postings a year. Back then, in a world where creative advertisement wasn't yet spread, one was something new and unique.

In the next few years, this new form of storytelling will change the world. More and more devices will connect to each other and monitor our body weight in real time, while sweatshirts will measure our temperature.

A shoe brand could object: 'Why should we care about digital technology? We can open an e-commerce website and sell 600 pairs a month of our 400 Euro shoes. This small online shop will cost 300,000 or 400,000 Euros, and our attached brand will testify that our shoes are made in high quality leather'. The problem is that competitors will come, possibly with no brand and no history, and they'll be able to radically transform our idea of a pair of shoes using a technology that measures an individual's steps or temperature and warns him when he's about to slip over something. Or these competitors' storytelling will be based on the value of wearing a pair of leather shoes that trace you while a life milestone happens to you and will remind you that you were in Paris when you first went out for a romantic dinner, or in Hong

Kong when you were interviewed for the job of your life. Just like Apple does with pictures, shoes could display a map of where your important life facts took place. A map showing where you and your pair of shoes were. This is what I call storytelling, because it centers around a customer.

Some brands prefer to tell about themselves. Think about Hamilton, the first wristwatch worn by American trainmen. But the people are Hamilton aren't telling me what their watches have done for me: they're telling me what Hamilton did for other people, who died a century ago.

The most important thing is to apply your storytelling to your customers. One of the great *insights* about products, and one of the reasons why advertisers work and consumers purchase, is our sense of belonging.

If I choose to buy an expensive shoe brand it's because I want people to know that I can afford them and I belong to a well-defined group. If my car is very expensive, I tend to conform to a set of behaviors. Therefore, in my case the *insight* may be my lack of self confidence.

We use brands both to belong to a group (the brand's group) and to hide behind that group's behavior. If I spend 1,000 Euros for a Hermes purse it means I can afford it. But this isn't enough anymore: Hermes and other similar brands work hard on craftsmanship, experience, history; they show us how their purses are made and why; they show us that Grace Kelly used to own a purse like ours. This is storytelling. When you wonder what the future of storytelling in the digital era is, think of devices being embedded into products. It may be not very Hermes-style but if your purse is equipped with a RFID tag (a radio-frequency identifier that communicates to other objects or transceivers) and every time you attend an event you're greeted in a special way because your purse is transmitting data about you, this is actually storytelling. Imagine your Armani shoes have a RFID tag and every time you walk into an Armani store anywhere in the world sales clerks recognize you as a loyal Armani customer, call you by your name and offer you a drink.

Some major fashion brands, notoriously very attentive to trends, are already doing that. Burberry is the most digitally advanced company in the fashion arena. Recently it spread some controversy because it was the first ever *maison* to get rid of *season collections*. So, no more yearly fashion shows to showcase the next season's collection. Burberry products on the catwalk are now immediately available for online purchase. Concepts such as autumn/winter and spring/summer are bypassed altogether, and you get one season with all clothes. If you want a specific garment, you can have it, now. This is a great chance for storytelling.

Prada has reacted: they haven't changed their positioning and kept the season collections, but they have opened a *ready-to-buy* channel. So when you attend a Prada fashion show you can instantly purchase an item you see.

This is what the digital novelization of a brand is all about: acknowledging you're in danger of disappearing and you need to make a digital change. Some brands (i.e., those that were born digital) have done this, others refuse to do it. But a way of digital storytelling exists for every brand. We covered some examples from the fashion world, a sector where brands are either very innovative or very tradition-based, but the same applies to food.

Picture a cookie brand with a lovely packaging featuring a QR code: we could use our smartphones to watch a video telling how the cookies were made, and where. It's not necessary to tell this story on TV. If the brand's imagery is based on a peculiar detail, such as a mill, it can be presented in a engagement-oriented way that tells its story differently. Having a corporate app is simply not enough, even though the company was very proud of launching it.

Having your own app is not innovation: it's adapting to the market. When you launch your own app you're not doing any digital business yet, you're simply adapting to a change that is imposed onto you from the outside. It's the least you can do if you want to survive.

If cookie companies are worried about kids growing fat after eating six cookies in a row, they should say so on their packaging. They should inform their mothers, but do it in a different way. Showing them a celebrity on TV is totally pointless. Television is only good when it comes to tell a brand's story and show its craftsmanship.

But what should cookie companies say on their packaging?

I want my cookies to tell me: 'Enough, Silvio. You've already eaten eight'.

I want my Church's shoes to tell my cookie pack I haven't walked enough to afford eight cookies. This is innovation. This is the new storytelling.

The world is rapidly transforming but many companies still have the same approach from 60 years ago. Either their management teams haven't yet singled out their products' specific placements and contexts (hence, their management teams need some changes) or companies are voluntarily committing suicide.

I believe that in 90% of circumstances managers tend to think backwards. They slightly adjust what they did the year before, so it's not their fault but the evolving market's if things go bad.

But you need to take some risks. You need to launch new products and use new ways to communicate. It's not something anyone can do: unfortunately, most brands are managed by people who don't own them and are judged by their performance. Hence, they tend to play it safe. The etymological root of the term 'entrepreneurship', which encompasses 'risk', has gone totally missing.

Innovation and change are an entrepreneur's thing. Leaving out-there visions aside (i.e., water companies selling weightless bottles that calm your thirst by simply watching them) and speaking of stories and how they can engage people, changes never happen *tout court.* Most Italian companies overlook this. But if a 'storytelling that helps adjusting a brand in a serious digital way' quadrant is missing from the whole picture, those companies must ask themselves why.

4.5 DON'T AIM AND MISS

Digital innovation allows us to predictively perform one of today's main marketing techniques: retargeting.

Unfortunately, it doesn't apply to everything though.

If you purchase a pair of Nike shoes for 60 Euros on Amazon, Amazon will soon tempt you with other colors of the same model and you may even fall for that. But if you're offered a smartphone or television after buying a smartphone or a TV set, Amazon (or any other service) is wasting your time and their money.

I can't believe that companies can't intercept this form of user discomfort; as a matter of fact, they're already spending money on retargeting.

In a shopping arcade or in a big mall, shop windows tend to change every two weeks or once a month. This is retargeting as well.

The difference is that a shopping window doesn't know I have already bought a suit.

A retargeting logic is very useful for companies when it comes to buying spaces that will be seen by their 'fans' and can be used to inform them and enrich their brand experience.

Think about a football team. It is usually a closed business (teams very rarely steal supporters from one another). The only retargeting a club can do is to sell me a pair of shorts that match the jersey I bought at the club's official store.

This mechanism can be easily adapted to e-commerce and it can be used to feed information to supporters.

A team, let's say Inter, can buy media spaces and only target Inter supporters by showing them that the next away game is going to be Juventus vs. Inter in Turin. A supporter/customer will be fed with: the weather forecast for the weekend in Turin, a selection of restaurants in Turin, a special offer on the train ticket to Turin, a map of parking places in Turin, a list of B&Bs in Turin.

Retargeting is a symbol for how poorly the huge potential of digital technology is taken advantage of. It only works if a company can create systems ensuring that, if a purchase has been completed, the purchaser does not receive further offers for the same product.

There's another process that companies, especially those in the media industry, have not yet fully embraced: attribution models. Attribution models allow a company to learn where a reader, a customer, a user exactly comes from. When you apply attribution models to the digital industry, the weight of what is really valuable is drastically different. The moment a company starts using an evolved attribution model, it radically changes.

In other words, it's all about learning how a user has reached your company. Here's an example: I'm tired and I'm casually watching an evening show on TV. A car commercial comes up and I go: 'Wow, I like that car'. Showing me that car is the only function TV should have. Even though I'm tired and careless and I don't want to interact any further, I grab my smartphone and 'google' the car model. I find an article about it: it features a request form for a test drive and I immediately fill it in. The following Saturday I'm at the test drive, I dig the car and I buy it. Now, according to less accurate analyses I have bought the car after my test drive, and this proves that test drives are what the car brand should invest in. However, if the people at the automotive company are good they'll know that the website article was crucial, because that's where I came from, and all the rest of the investment should be cancelled, including the TV ads. But this way the company would never acquire any new customers. However, if attribution analyses are truly complete, they'll prove that the TV commercial was my starting point. This is a very important fact to ponder, as managers are always on the look for investments that can be cut. Wrongfully cancelling a proper investment is against any company's interests.

Attribution models are a form of big data (which we'll thoroughly discuss later) and can be of two types: one is the 'econometric model', allowing businesses to manage their own *media overall* (that is, across all channels, both online and offline) instead of outsourcing it to a media agency. Using extremely evolved and trustworthy software an in-house analyst can find the proper media mix that allows investors not only to reach their saturation curve (the maximum number of sales you can get from a given investment) but also to calculate their brand's weight.

As we're consistently and increasingly going digital, some attribution systems that are connected to social platforms (Facebook) can distribute a company's investment across the digital chain in a more appropriate and optimized way.

For instance, Facebook can learn if my online purchase or visit at a shop originates from an ad that I saw while I was chatting on my profile. Those who'll miss the wealth of opportunities that attribution models can offer in our increasingly larger media market are bound to lose a lot of money.

4.6 THE MORE YOU TELL, THE MORE I KNOW: *CURATORS* AND **THE NEW STORYTELLING**

Luigino is the owner of a grocery shop in Milan. If walk into his shop and have a lovely chat with him, you'll immediately realize he has nothing to do with the grocery stall worker at your regular mall, the one who's usually trying to sell you more ham or cheese than you actually need.

Luigino buys his products from farms – that's why they cost twice the price at a supermarket – and he can tell you what he's selling to you, where it comes from, who made it and how. I used to have a similar experience at Fnac: there was a guy at the music department who was a real expert of anything music-related, he knew *everything*. That experience was pretty meaningful to me. To someone like me, who loves music but struggles to pay one Euro to download a single song from iTunes, that interaction made great sense. The same happened at another record shop I used to go to in Milan: I spent hours talking with the shop assistant there. For users like me Spotify is not enough. An algorithm can't (yet) provide the kind of service I treasure. **I like both Verdi and Mahler, but the Spotify algorithm can only suggest me**

either one of the two. It cannot perform a *connoisseur*'s job, he cannot be an expert explaining me things drawing from *his own* verifiable knowledge.

Also, sound quality is miles away from what I get from an analog medium. I don't use music as a background, which is the purpose Spotify was invented for. When I listen to music I want to do it using the best equipment and in the highest quality: I want it to be an experience.

A simple *stream of consciousness*, Spotify is also biased by record companies, because you can't really find everything. It's very similar to another of my hobbies: Wikipedia. Sometimes I go there to look up something and let myself be caught up. I follow the hypertexts and spend half an hour without even recalling why I got there in the first place. But I have flicked through a couple of things I didn't know anything about, which is good. Well, Spotify provides a similar experience to me.

Here's another example: let's say I'm in a town I've never been to and I want to have dinner at a *nice* place. At first I'm tempted – because it's the first result the Google algorithm returns – to follow a link from TripAdvisor, a tool that was apparently invented to fulfill this specific need. However, when you stop and think about how TripAdvisor works, some obvious limitations emerge, for the restaurant/company and the user/consumer alike.

Here's why. On the same evening, A and B have dinner at the same restaurant: A is not happy and gives a star out of five, while B has a great dining experience and gives the restaurant five stars.

Who's right? Both are.

If we filter out the raving reviews by the chef's own relatives and the bashings by the owners of the restaurants on the other side of the road, A and B's reviews are written by common people with diametrically opposed evaluations. This goes to show that a tool that is so open to masses can't be trusted. We all have our own preferences.

One thing can be perceived or interpreted in two opposing ways by two different people, as a famous split screen scene from Woody Allen's *Annie Hall* funnily shows (a psychoanalyst asks a couple how often they have sex: Diane Keaton goes 'Constantly. I'd say three times a week', Woody Allen replies 'Hardly ever. Maybe three times a week').

So if you're looking for a trustworthy review you'll need someone with a face, a name and a surname, a food or catering expert with some

175

culinary culture, who is paid to do their job. In other words, the service offered by TripAdvisor is pointless and you should rely on high end guides such as *Michelin* or *Gambero Rosso*, where reviews are written by cuisine experts who do this for a living.

However, sometimes experts pose a serious bias risk that advertisers know very well: *scams*. A famous chef advertising an appliance brand is not giving an expert's suggestion. He's saying something he would have said for *any* another brand, it's just a matter of which brand pays the highest fee. It's not dissimilar from what Elio, a satirical Italian singer, used to sarcastically say *before* every concert: 'You're an amazing audience, I'll never stop saying this to you, and to the those who came to all our other gigs'. An expert's suggestion will always be worthless as long as companies pay experts to say what they want them to concept of *advocates*, as long as they don't realize that social channels such as TripAdvisor allowed chaos to break loose. **There's only one role that actually ought to exist: a *curator*. Somebody who personally vouches for quality, which is something that very few brands do today.** Some social channels with an editorial line exist and their goal is to raise their readers' level, with quality contents curated by people who really know things.

One example is Italian publisher Einaudi, whose Twitter channel has become a true reference for book lovers.

Einaudi's tweets don't necessarily agree with users to convince them to buy a book, but drive genuine, unbiased discussions about literature, writers and writing.
The account is managed by an expert who acts like somebody

'YOU'RE AN AMAZING AUDIENCE,
I'LL NEVER STOP SAYING THIS TO YOU, AND TO THE THOSE WHO CAME TO ALL OUR OTHER GIGS'

_Elio e le storie tese

'who knows things' and is hence entitled to give suggestions, just like an old-school librarian. But things can also be much easier: a few years ago Walmart set up a network allowing users to chat with a dedicate shop assistant from anywhere in the world.

When you flip the binoculars over, everything looks small.

Let's start from the end. Until some years ago, a term was very popular and trendy: *bespoke*, or *tailor made.* Nike even made a portal where users could make their own version of a shoe (this approach was quickly dropped when it proved unsustainable, though). If a brand could advise single consumers after listening to them, and then synthesize their requests using a bot, they could get amazing benefits.

A *curator* is the starting point for the next form of storytelling.

Some US companies incorporate actual agencies that manage their brand and the whole communication chain. A *curator* is a sort of editor here, a crossbreed between a marketing office manager and a troubadour.

This role already exists at brands that curate their editorial profile. But sooner or later all mediators will be bypassed.

For mass market products, the term *curator* is probably too far-fetched (it comes from art, after all), but it's a concept that can be easily introduced, with all due distinctions.

The only way Swiss watchmakers can survive massification is by telling their century-old stories, which is the only thing that distinctively differentiates them from the Silicon Valley giants. If you have a look at *any* project presentation on Kickstarter you'll notice that they all tell a product's story or show how perfectly its features can adapt to a user.

This is what I call 'second-level storytelling', this is *curating*. It allows to exactly define the people a company is targeting with its products. People want to hear stories, brands want to tell them.

When a housewife stands at a supermarket shelf – the 'first moment of truth' as P&G calls it – she'll pick your product because of its story.

Your product, and its story.

Picked among many others, in a blink.

Chapter 5

WE LOVE SHOPPING

5.1 A NEW WAY OF PURCHASING

5.2 USER EXPERIENCE **AS A DIVINE LAW**

5.3 ENHANCING YOUR RESULTS VIA **CRM AND BIG DATA**

5.4 CHANGING BEHAVIORS

5.5 KEEPING UP WITH **THE TIMES**

5.6 WE'RE OUR OWN **SHOP ASSISTANTS**

5.7 YOUR SMARTPHONE: A REMOTE CONTROL FOR SHOPPING

5.1 A NEW WAY **OF PURCHASING**

When we're asked to make some quick free associations with the words 'United States of America', we generally come up with the usual things: the stars and stripes flag, the White House, cheeseburgers and soda drinks, green bills with old Presidents on them. Some of us may add Hollywood, Wall Street, Trump. Or the Silicon Valley, the Rust Belt, the first man on the Moon. And, inevitably, New York.

Everybody knows the 'city that doesn't sleep', even those who've never been there. We all know it from books and short stories. It's the backdrop and sometimes the leading character of countless movies and TV series. At least once a year, on a mid September day, we all symbolically join its citizens in honoring the victims of terrorism.

The Statue of Liberty, the Empire State Building, Central Park and Times Square are universal symbols. Either on actual foot or with our imagination, we all have walked down Fifth Avenue, the world's most famous shopping street.

On this 10-kilometer street you'll find the most expensive flat rents in the world. In the stretch between Thirty-fourth and Fifty-ninth streets, you'll witness it in its full glory: a long parade of stores on both sidewalks, the Earth's most famous brands, make this the ultimate 'shopping street' outshining London's Oxford Street or the Champs-Élysées in Paris.

Here's the thing, though: with its glittering shop windows, Fifth Avenue is more European than American. New York City itself has nothing to do with the rest of the States: it actually looks like an European super city transplanted into the States. Thinking of New York and its shopping avenue when asked about America is basically a common place, and it's wrong.

99% of the USA has nothing to do with New York and its branded retail stores.

Normal City is a 55,000-people town in the middle of Illinois, a 2-hour drive from Chicago. It is twinned, among others, with Nazareth in Israel and Canterbury in the UK.

It is home of the Illinois State University, where David Foster Wallace served as a Professor from 1993 to 2002. This town – as it name suggests – is exemplarily normal. It perfectly showcases how shopping 'the American way' works. On its whole surface of about 50 square kilometers – with a density of 1,100 inhabitants per square kilometer – you won't find a shopping district. There's no European-style 'shopping avenue' in Normal City.

To do their shopping, citizens go to the town's two malls and fulfill most of their needs in an ad hoc place protected from the weather, while air conditioning and a free Wi-Fi connection cuddle them all along their experience. They can buy polo shirts and chino trousers at Tommy Hilfiger, pant suits at Ann Taylor and Dress Barn, phone subscriptions at Verizon, a vanilla Frappuccino at Starbucks; they can rent a car at Enterprise, buy shampoos and bath salts at Bath and Body Works, and find pretty anything – at a sale price – at Target.

All of this is super standard, 'super normal'.

So think of Normal City, not New York, next time you try picturing the real USA.

The United States have a population of more than 325 million people, making it the third most populated country in the world, behind China and India. Also, the States are the fourth biggest country on Earth. The population is very unevenly distributed. Its average density is of 34 inhabitants per square kilometer, which is a remarkable amount when compared to Italy and San Marino, totaling 206 and 500 people per square kilometer respectively.

A Texan living at a 1.5 hour drive from the nearest ranch – this is not a hyperbole, but an average – will think twice before hopping on his pickup truck and driving to the shopping mall when it's 99°F in the shade. Sure, he'll do it every now and then, but not on a regular basis. In San Francisco, shopping isn't the most popular of sports. It soon gets boring, because you soon realize you'll find the same flagship stores by the same brands over and over: Ralph Lauren, Tommy Hilfiger, Abercrombie...

Before e-commerce, people from Normal as well as most Americans had only one alternative to shopping-malls: the catalogs they received with the mail.

When I was living in the States, opening the mailbox every day was a feast for my daughters. Here in Italy my mailbox is usually pretty empty, and when I think back at the one I had in the US I tend to become melancholic. I only get some letters here, usually from my electricity supplier or bank – actually not anymore, since I have recently switched to online invoicing and bank statements – and the occasional parking or speeding ticket. It's quite depressing. When we were living in America, my daughters would rush outside to collect our mail because they knew they would find a catalog, a cent from a fund reminding us to invest or some other gift. They would come back to the house with their hands full of parcels. I still have mail being delivered to my San Francisco house and the current tenant keeps it for me month after month (except for the catalogs, that would require a separate bookcase), while UPS still ships heaps of letters to that address.

To replace catalogs we invented e-commerce, and that's why in the States an online assortment of products is still called a 'catalog'.

Some paper catalogs are actually amazing, they're just like coffee table books. They're great to read when you're in bed. They're like magazines, books, art objects.

When I was working at HP, we would dispatch 15 million catalogs to our customers three times a year, and yet it was nothing compared to what other companies were doing. To make catalogs companies generally hire some dedicated staff, professionals who know what to place on the front page, on page 2 and so on and of people who are very good at storytelling. It is an actual in-house publishing enterprise, planned to the tiniest detail, pretty refined, medium-to-high level.

The USA are experiencing a percentage increase of e-commerce purchases against the total amount of retail: 8.1% (over 97 billion dollars) in the second quarter of 2016.[15]

In 2015 the online sale of products and services had reached 7.4% of total retail sales globally: 1,671 billion dollars, a 350 billion dollars increase from 2014.

By 2019, the amount will be more than doubled and reach 3,578 billion dollars. According to Emarketer, it will still be a fraction (12.8%) of total retail purchases, though.

---

[15] Source: http://www2.census.gov/retail/releases/historical/ecomm/16q2.pdf

5.2 USER EXPERIENCE **AS A DIVINE LAW**

According to a recent study,[16] 76% of Italians make an online search before purchasing. Before making a decision, an average of 5.4 different information sources are consulted and 71% of them are online. Also, 47% of Italians use their smartphones even when they're at a retail point.

In Italy, e-commerce has changed the way products are sold, especially when it comes to customer care. We use e-commerce because we've learned that is pretty convenient: the delivery of what we need is just a click away. The estimated value of e-commerce turnover in Italy in 2015 was about 28.8 billion Euros, marking a 19% growth from 2014.[17] 'Leisure time' and 'Tourism' sectors rule the roost, covering 30% and 47% of the market respectively.

Also, this experience has drastically changed relationships with customers.

Consider item returns: in the past, when you returned a product, the

---

[16] Gianluca Diegoli, minimarketing.it
[17] Source: https://www.casaleggio.it/wp-content/uploads/2016/04/Focus_E-commerce_2016_Web1.pdf

best you could hope for was a voucher, that you had to spend at the same shop and within a fixed timeframe. At the dawn of e-commerce some frauds took place, but things quickly got better. Rip-offs and scams are now very rare, because once sellers are reported to site moderators they're thrown out.

For sellers, the first mistake is also the last. e-commerce may have pushed some (offline) shops out of business, but it has also quickly regulated the online market. Amazon's return policy has become the Internet

IN ITALY, E-COMMERCE HAS CHANGED THE WAY PRODUCTS ARE SOLD, ESPECIALLY WHEN IT COMES TO CUSTOMER CARE: PEOPLE ARE MEDIA

standard, and those who don't comply are perceived in a negative way. Amazon allows you to return not only the damaged, faulty, non-functioning products but also those you don't like or need; all of it at its own expense, and with a full money refund. A revolutionary service for Italy, a country where if you buy a suit at a shop and it rips up when you first wear it the blame will be automatically on you and you'll need a lawyer to have a portion of your money back.

Until recently, sales clerks at consumer electronics retailers were experts who could give you informed suggestions. **Today's clerks are**

mostly there to prevent people from stealing or to show them the exit sign or a shelf. They're inexperienced because they've had some poor and unprofessional training. This is a bad thing because they won't develop any affection for their job: in the best case scenario they're barely legal trainees, who'll give you information about a product by reading its tag with you, for the first time.

It happens every time: you go to a megastore to buy a vacuum cleaner or another appliance and ask a clerk for advice and you get a reply that would make any psychology and marketing expert happy: 'This model you're looking at is very good, I have the same model at home'.

Apparently, in Italy every clerk working in every shop owns the very same model of vacuum cleaner, washing machine and television that a customer is looking at any given time.

Some time ago I needed to buy a new beard trimmer. Over the course of my life I have tried all brands and all types of trimmers, collecting all kinds of scams in the process. So I went to Amazon and decided not to look for brands, but for user reviews. In the end, I picked a brand, which I won't mention, that I recalled being the first I had ever used. It had plenty of positive reviews.

Other people's reviews are like a certification to me and the same applies to many online buyers; you can even ask specific questions to users who have already purchased a product. You ask other consumers, not the company that manufactured the product.

In many sectors, users purchase because they're 'guided' by suggestions by influencers and other individuals they feel they can trust because they're 'just like them', or at least this is what they believe.[18] **Influencers are not celebrities 'per se', they're celebrities in their own fields, because this is where they've built their credibility.** Before purchasing a product such as a smartphone or a car, a common user tends to consult an expert's opinion in the form of a trustworthy review on a specialized website or on YouTube.

Differently, when users want to know about the latest videogame, they tend to trust their peers and exchange opinions with them on dedicated community forums.[19]

---

[18] Source: Nielsen/inPowered MediaLab study, December 2013-January 2014
[19] Source: https://www.inpwrd.com/the_role_of_content_inpowered.pdf

5.3 ENHANCING YOUR RESULTS VIA CRM AND BIG DAT

According to CRM Academy, when people are in a state of neglect, they tend to tell the truth. That's why, **when users unsubscribe from their newsletters, many American brands email them a form asking for the reason.** Amazon does the same when a user cancels an order. It happens because these companies know that people tend to be honest in such circumstances, while they might lie when they fall in love with a brand or product. Why should I purchase something? I need a reason to do it, for instance my wish to buy someone a present. But when I don't complete my order, I tend to tell the truth: 'I won't buy it because your prices are too high!', 'It doesn't work!'. Brands really need to learn this kind of information. Perhaps Italians don't like being criticized. We have a culture for 'false kindness'. As a matter of fact, our main issue is our ignorance, in a literal sense, the fact that we 'ignore' things. Companies realize a phenomenon is taking place but their managers are ignorant, they ignore how to handle it or how they can efficiently react. In Italy, a CEO and a Marketing Director will simply say something like: 'Do we have a social page? Post something.' Companies release apps that get very low ratings (one star out of five) but they won't change a thing. The truth is that if your app gets one out of five stars, there is a problem with it. Whether you're a product or a service provider, if you get such a low rating you should withdraw your app, try and understand why it performed so badly and improve it until it gets a better result.

Interacting with businesses is such an easy thing today: the company that makes the chocolate I eat every morning is just a click away. It's as quick as clicking 'Send message' on their Facebook page. And if I want to call them, I just need to look up their website and I'll find the number. The same applies if I want to email them. CRM (Customer Relationship Management) can help even the most unprepared customer today.

By managing their relationship with the people who buy their products, companies can certainly increase loyalty but they also risk making mistakes

WHEN PEOPLE ARE IN A STATE OF NEGLECT, THEY TEND TO TELL THE TRUTH

that can spoil everything. More than anything else, they need a strategy that goes beyond technologies and answers; a proper strategy must comprise all the necessary steps and be able to thoroughly analyze a customer's environment. Every corporate process must be monitored and become a part of a complex system committed to a company's relationship with people. This applies to both B2B and B2C. There's no doubt that companies need to log and analyze their interactions with those who buy their goods or services, but to be of any use such analyses must get out of their PowerPoint presentations and help them evolve via user suggestions.

A wrong strategy can make even the best software fail. And speaking of tools, they're pretty easy to find today. Companies can use the traditional tools we have mentioned above, or they can rely on online chats, forums, chatbots, FAQs, Twitter as a CRM instrument and many other features that new technologies provide every day.

And yet many companies equipped with open customer relation channels still hardly give answers or they reply in an unprepared manner.

Companies need to stop expecting that users will spontaneously come to them and tell them what's wrong. Thank God many of them still do (and companies should give them a thank as big as their reputation), but the truth is that people increasingly tend to comment restaurants on TripAdvisor, hotels on Booking.com, products on Facebook and services on forums and blogs. Companies need to interact with these people through a new CRM system that is ready to correct or fine-tune their communications and is also highly responsive, in order to log all reports and send them to their management teams. Companies will need to do so if they want to grow and evolve, otherwise their competitors will win over them almost effortlessly. Only big and structured companies currently act like this. Yet it would be very useful to small enterprises, as they could use such insights to surpass their competitors. Every concern, suggestion or complaint by a user must be incorporated in a long-term strategy aimed at improving a company's relationship with a customer. Not a generic customer, but a 'specific' customer. When Marco C. posts that he's purchased an excellent smartphone but doesn't know how to upgrade its memory, he's pointing out a need that demands an immediate response. But it also implies that he may be open to an extra option, such as replacing his current smartphone with a model with a greater storage memory. If companies want to identify every single user, not as a type but as an actual individual (or a company, in the case of B2B relationships), they need to either promote personal relationships at stores (but opening a store chain implies high expenses and not-so-high incomes) or start logging and analyzing everything, person by person.

Performing a good CRM means collecting data and, much earlier than we think, it'll mean collecting *big data*. Some companies have already started scanning their users via much more sophisticated tools than a simple questionnaire or a list of performed actions.The goal here is to try and define a customer's preferences, both on the monitored system and in real everyday life. That's why smartphone applications become a key factor, as they allow users to get anything they need with a click and also log their preferences, visited places, interactions and much more. And they do all of this for a brand.

Using collected data, companies will learn a user's every single trait and need: if they know a user's habits, they can be ready to ensure a better service. This way, the information that companies periodically send to customers (offer leaflets, activity summary documents) could be highly customized according to a single consumer's requirements and preferred purchases. Be warned, though: it's not just a matter of promoting a new offer for a professional, wishing them happy birthday, notifying them that a bank branch office is closed, or offering a discount because they're loyal customers.
It's a matter of deeply learning their habits so that a company can ensure every single user gets either the best possible offer or an ad hoc price. Think about electricity suppliers: today, very few of them ensure

customized offers and for a very limited number of customers, usually big companies with high power consumptions.

A consultant visits one of such companies, learns all their needs, assesses the numbers, creates a document filled with information and figures, hands it to the company manager

PERFORMING A GOOD CRM MEANS COLLECTING DATA AND, MUCH EARLIER THAN WE THINK, IT WILL MEAN COLLECTING BIG DATA

who analyzes it, makes his own calculations and so on. In the end, the company manager believes he's gotten a discount, the consultant gains his percentage fee, the supplier is happy because they have acquired a new big customer. But this cumbersome process is unthinkable of with small B2C clients, that is us, the common people, because the gain margin for a company and its consultants is too low for such a huge waste of time. And we all know that time is money. Big data will allow us to have a smart algorithm calculating the best possible ad hoc offer for a family man with two children and a wife, three televisions and four mobile phones, a pc and two laptops, a number of electric appliances. He won't need to choose from the countless offers he'll find online and he won't have to suffer a call center operator offering him a supply plan he has already subscribed to. During the call he'll be told about a specific offer, or he'll get it via email or in a SMS message or app notification. The company that can best analyze the daily habits of the prospect's family will win. To do so, the company needs all available data: the number of mobile phones, their recharging speed, the passion for music and stereo equipment or television, the wish to purchase new appliances or technological devices. **All of this will impact call centers as we know them.** We'll stop getting calls at every time of day, done by operators who hardly know our name. Their generic answers will disappear with them. The service will not go away altogether, though; as a matter of fact, it will survive but in a different form. As we'll increasingly get used to a higher level service for our purchases and offers (the 'Amazon' way we discussed earlier), we'll expect to get a premium service also when it comes to handling our concerns and issues. Currently, call centers are either basic services outsourced abroad for saving purposes or second-level internal services addressing a small élite of lucky customers. Only the latter will survive, because the former will be replaced by artificial intelligence or other computers.

Relying on a high quality CRM service will soon be a plus, and it's already a strength point for some companies.

5.4 CHANGING BEHAVIORS

People in communication know what messages can give and 'make people do'. For some, the goal of any communication idea is to make people change their behaviors: a message should convince you to do something in a way that is different from what you were ready or inclined to do. Most probably, the most ambitious achievement a company can aim at is to change your behavior.

Within the digital scenario this can be done in a way that won't make you feel it is being imposed from the top. You'll believe you're making an autonomous choice.

When I turn on my TV, a commercial suggests me to buy 'Detergent X'. If I later purchase 'Detergent X', I may think for a fraction: 'What a sucker I am: I bought it because television told me so!' The nice thing about digital technology is that it'll make me buy 'Detergent X' and I won't realize, because its persuasion acts differently. It's like reading a newspaper article with some advertisement in it; they call it 'native advertising'. A company gives me a nice piece that says good things about something or feeds me some contents I'm interested in via a

Facebook post or a friend's suggestion. There's a whole set of methods a company can use to change and steer my behavior. Once ascertained that my needs and habits have changed, it's essential for products and brands to surpass their competitors in the real moment of truth: when my finger is on the 'Purchase' button.

5.5 KEEPING UP WITH THE TIMES

The times have changed, and society has become less hedonistic than it used to be: people have learned how to better spend their money, and maybe even how to spend less. **What is the future of communication within our historical context?** The word 'better' does not go well with our old ways of communicating. If an ad tells you 'Buy Product X, use Product X', it doesn't necessarily imply 'Spend better'. Today, 'spending better' means a user types 'best washing machine detergent' on Google so that an algorithm can bring up a test demonstrating Product X's efficacy in terms of chemical reactions on a molecular level. This way, that user will be convinced that Product X is better and he'll believe he's found out by himself.

On a behavioral level, we can say that digital technology has filled the 'cultural shopping' gap that Italy used to have compared to other countries, especially the USA.

Think about the things you've recently purchased online and consider for how many of them you made a prior research and read other users' comments and reviews before buying. All of them? Does this mean that the millions of Euros invested on advertising last year were spent in vain? Today, when you need a new washing machine, you compare all technical performance data, read all the reviews and acquire all the details you need to make your choice. You shop with a deeper awareness, or at least that's what you believe. True 'word of mouth' has always existed in the USA, much earlier than in Europe and on the Internet. When it comes to shopping, Europeans are less inclined to sociality and sharing than Americans. Here a product's endorsement is very limited, unless it's a fashion item. In such a case, consumers tend to show off their purchases. They won't tell or describe much about them, though. And even if they did, others would remain pretty indifferent.

Once, we used to go to a store when we needed to buy an appliance. Things have drastically changed today. On the one hand, **it's not essential anymore to see a physical item before buying it.** The old Bedouin golden rule – 'Show money, see camel' – does not apply to e-commerce. In my personal experience, I have bought a Prada belt after viewing it on my smartphone. I saw the price, the alternatives and then asked myself: 'Why should I go to a store and waste my time? This is the current collection and it won't change, regardless of my physical presence. I'll buy it online and have it delivered at home'. The same happened when I purchased a keyboard for my iPad: I was on the underground and googled 'best keyboard iPad mini'. Once I found the best model and its store price (100 Euros), I went to Amazon, found out that I could pay 44 Euros (including delivery) for a refurbished (or reconditioned) model, and bought it.

Traditional shops can't compete with that. If they don't evolve by adapting to this scenario, they'll die. Shop owners as we know them will

THE ONLY REAL MOMENT OF TRUTH:
THE 'PURCHASE' BUTTON

soon be extinct, whatever bad and traumatic this may sound to those who work in retail. *The Anarchist Cookbook* is a book from the Seventies that was banished from the US because it fundamentally taught people how to build their own weapons and synthesize their own drugs.[20] Here's a passage from the introduction: 'This book is for the people of the United States of America. It is not written for the members of fringe political groups (…). Those radical groups don't need this book. They already know everything that's in here. If the real people of America, the silent majority, are going to survive, they must educate themselves. That is the purpose of this book'. In our own little way, we're saying the same things and for the same reason.

---

[20] William Powell, The Anarchist Cookbook, Ozark Pr Llc, s.l. 1971

5.6 WE'RE OUR OWN **SHOP ASSISTANTS**

Once we were in a meeting with a very important client, and we realized we had to include a 'Hobby' category in our database, so that we could improve our knowledge of their customers by receiving relevant and up-to-date behavioral details.

We ended up dropping 'Cinema', which was a too generic and misleading category (people who only watch love stories starring TV celebrities and people who only watch art movies in original language cannot be in the same pool), and adding 'e-commerce'. e-commerce is in fact a 'hobby': we spend hours fantasizing about objects, getting inspirations on Instagram and Pinterest, envisioning our next house, next car, next haircut.

We change our minds, ceaselessly, and digital technology allows us to do so. We add and remove items from our shopping carts all the time. Sometimes our hobby stops here. Compared to the total value of American trade, digital technology has simply moved the act of purchasing from one (physical) channel to another (digital). **For years, advertisers have inured consumers to get on their cars, drive for**

miles while fantasizing about the things they were about to buy, and finally reach a store where they could fulfill their wish to purchase. Let's be honest, though: when Italians go to a shopping mall, they'll only find a replica of a lifestyle model they're very familiar with, something they can easily experience in their town's shopping street. If they live in big cities this will only come to a higher cost in terms of time.

But let's assume for a moment I'll get on my car and go somewhere to do my shopping, with a budget.

I'll most probably do something foolish. 'I have made something foolish' was quite a common expression back in the day, meaning you had started a purchase process out of impulse, driven by a shop assistant's ability to convince you that you needed to match your pair of shoes with a briefcase and an extra pair of shoes.

It certainly also happens with e-commerce: merchants try to cross-sell and up-sell all the time, they tell users that their black shoes need black belts; but if a merchant can successfully inure users online, why should users go to its retail shop? They'll comfortably stay at home, order what they need and spend the time they've saved doing something else.

According to the *MetaPack 2016: State of eCommerce Delivery Consumer*

Research Report, [21] 90% of Italians are satisfied with their most recent online purchase, while less than 20% have had a negative experience in their online shopping in the last 12 months. For 87% of respondents a positive shopping experience acts as an encouragement to make other online purchases. 72% buy multiple items with a single shopping cart to be entitled to a free delivery, which seems to be an essential discriminating parameter for Italian online consumers.

The need for premium services with ultra-fast delivery times is growing. Requests for loyalty programs are particularly high (87% of total consumers). In general, 57% of respondents are satisfied with the services they get from online stores.

Traditional shops won't disappear soon, though, and that's because the possibility of discovering and emotionally connecting to objects is still strongly tied to the physical world. Digital technology is great for compensating and extending the human voice. Customers still need a strong experience. An e-commerce website with a nice layout and an invitation to 'buy online because it's cheaper' is simply not enough. In a selected number of cities around the world Adidas has opened special stores for running lovers called *Runbase*. Here you can find advice for

---

[21] The full report can be downloaded at: http://www.metapack.com/2016-state-of-ecommerce-delivery/

your next marathon or everyday training and you can use the store premises as your base for your running sessions, or to take a shower. You can also have your measures taken to make a custom insole that matches your top-of-the-line shoes, but those shoes cannot be purchased at a *Runbase* store. This example shows that you always have to ensure your customers enjoy a real-life experience (even if the follow-up is an online purchase), because this is a habit that won't be easily eradicated and probably won't ever be.

When I was younger, I used to go to London to buy my Dr Martens boots and shoes. They were not being sold in Italy: you could only get them in London and owning a pair made you 'cool', exclusive, original because it meant you had bought it in London.

Today, I can buy a pair of Dr Martens anywhere. There's even a competitor that allows me to customize my shoes in a thousand different ways. Not so long ago people went crazy for 'bespoke' items. Bespoke products are out of fashion now, because they've been made accessible to everybody. The satisfaction you get from having something that was tailor-made for you has lost the aura of uniqueness that once made it so attractive.

Prada competitors are not only Zegna, Dior and all the other high end fashion brands that own a flagship store in the via Monte Napoleone area known as Milan's 'Quadrilatero della Moda' (fashion quadrilateral), an actual and exclusive *open-air luxury mall*.

Their competitors are a number of 'cool' brands whose coolness has nothing to do with luxury: they're cool because they belong to the world of exclusive 'bespoke' items, a small universe of fake craftsmanship, fake sustainability, New Zealand businesses that only make clothes from albino veal leather, African businesses that try and imitate the crazy new US economy by only selling online, but from Kenya.

All these niches exist, and these brands are as cool as Zegna, because their belts cost 200 Euros. They have become the new heralds of luxury. Their uniqueness only lies in the fact that you can only reach them if you know about them. **In the past you had to know all the cool shops, now you need to know all the cool websites, which is essentially the same thing.**

The Web is filled with portals such as *The Fab* sending out mailing lists of recommendations from all over the world. The rise of digital technology has paved the way for an outbreak of niche products that couldn't find a distributor and now have become easily available. Once, if you had invented a portable umbrella, you needed to visit all reseller chains to demonstrate your product, and they would often reject it.

Today, not only retail chains are struggling to survive, but all these steps have been bypassed by digital technology. If your product is good or has some distinctive features, if it has a nice design or makes people feel good for some reason, if it is somehow unique or there's some peculiar quality to it, then it has a good chance of being sold, regardless of your marketing skills and your ability to promote it and show it around.

IN THE PAST YOU HAD TO KNOW ALL THE COOL SHOPS, NOW YOU NEED TO KNOW ALL THE COOL WEBSITES

You may even manage to sell it by yourself, with no middle-people; or you can use Amazon or eBay.

All of this is amazing, because it brings about an unbelievable democratization.

Digital technology has had three major effects on selling strategies:

1) Paying less is better than paying more. It may seem obvious, but that's what it is. Amazon got it before anybody else: they made an app

that allows you to scan the barcode of any product with your smartphone. If you walk into a bookstore and scan any book, the app will display its price on Amazon. Which is obviously lower. After all, researches confirm that 90% of consumers visit Amazon before buying a product anywhere else; 55% of online searches for products starts from Amazon.[22] So, here's the first thing: paying less is better than paying more. I feel terribly sorry for the shops, for their shop clerks, I feel sorry for everyone, but that's how it is.

2) I generally look for quality products, so I read all the reviews and available comparative tests. I invest my time on it and I gather that low quality products are bound to disappear from the market. However, you also need to remember that a product's quality is a user's decision, so providing quality means fulfilling the demand of a specific user who's buying a specific product.

We're talking about a niche user, someone whose clear and exhaustive review can convince others that are just like him. In the past, I would go to a shop and trust the clerk: if he had had no trouble with a brand, he would most probably recommend it to me and I would buy it. In e-

---

[22] 55% of online product searches begin on Amazon: stats – 27/09/2016 -
https://www.clickz.com/55of-online-product-searches-begin-on-amazon-stats/106326/?utm_
source=ClickZ+Global&utm_campaign=e0948d5d42-28_09_2016_NL&utm_medium=email&utm_
term=0_33e702b796-e0948d5d42-17834001

commerce, if somebody has had an issue with a product, the product's ranking drops so low that it will most probably never sell another unit anymore. So quality pays, at least what end users perceive as such.

3) Everything is in a user's hands. So, since our preferences are limitless and products are countless, we can fulfill our demands, always and anytime. The truth about us is stored in our browser cache memory.

When it comes to digital technology, the process of purchasing looks like a psychoanalysis session. Recently, I went to Puglia for my holidays: it is a most amazing place but, if I have to be honest, I was a bit fed up in the end. The year before I had stayed at a holiday farm in Tuscany. I liked it better, mainly because I don't like overcrowded places. Each one of us has their own preferences, you know. And this is good, otherwise we'd all go to the same place and there wouldn't be room for everybody.

We all love different things. Some love to go to New York on a summer holiday and they would never swap it with a tropical beach, because they simply hate beaches. But most people love exotic beaches, so everybody's happy at the end of the day.

This theory applies to purchasing: I have bought a specific car model because I needed it for my family; my wife agreed on it because she felt confident driving it. A whole decision flow unravels when it comes to purchasing and recently it has significantly extended. Most of all, the digital memories of my devices know everything about me: not only the choices I've made (they're plain to see: anybody can see what car I own and where I love to go on holiday), but also those that I haven't made.

The whole purchasing process happens digitally and my computer holds the researches I have made, the car model I started from. My computer can tell you that I visited the Mercedes website and used their online configurator on one of their most expensive models, but eventually purchased a Fiat Freemont. My browser and my mobile phone cache memories have stored what I really wanted to do. They can show you what holiday I wished I had made. They'll tell you I browsed through some farms and places in Umbria, but eventually picked a seaside village in Puglia, because that's where I had to go. But for a little while I fantasized, I spent some time looking for something else. When I bought my Venice house my budget was very limited, but I enjoyed browsing through the 1-million terraced lofts anyway. I looked at the ancient frescoed buildings overlooking the Grand Canal even if I could never afford them. And my computer knows about it, because everything is stored in its cache memory. There lies the list of all our true wishes.

5.7 YOUR SMARTPHONE: **A REMOTE CONTROL FOR SHOPPING**

Television is still anchored to a passive fruition model. Once it is integrated with contents, it will evolve into smart television. You'll have travel documentaries allowing you to book your next holidays, a MasterChef episode with an option to buy groceries, a movie such as *The Devil Wears Prada* with a jewelers offer. **My smartphone is already a remote control allowing me to switch channels, to record programs and to do whatever I want to.**

Currently, TV programs don't allow a higher interaction because channels are still static, but they're being enhanced by SMS and tweet interactions and voting options during live shows and live streams.

A further step forward, not too distant from our current everyday life, will be using smartphones to purchase what you see on your first screen.

The future of shopping is interactive shopping. The future of viewing is interactive viewing. They go hand in hand and they'll allow us to enjoy some truly immersive experiences. A good example comes from the porn industry, which is taking some giant steps in the augmented reality scenario. The whole porn industry is becoming increasingly 'virtual': from hardware, with dolls that look like living people and wireless dildos, to a mix of augmented and virtual reality that will allow users to have sex with their favorite porn stars. The experience will seem so real much that we'll end up wondering whether this is actually cheating on our partners. Back to more ordinary things, our mobile phone will allow us to enjoy virtual reality experiences during our everyday life., with extra videos, interviews and travelling suggestions.

We'll be able to know everything about a product in a shop, we'll get all the info we need about some lovely orange we're about to buy at the supermarket, we'll watch a TV documentary about Kenya

THE FUTURE OF SHOPPING IS INTERACTIVE SHOPPING, THE FUTURE OF VIEWING IS INTERACTIVE VIEWING

safari tours and immediately get all the info about the place, with extra videos, interviews and travelling suggestions. But we'll be able to do much more. While watching a safari documentary we'll be able to buy the Masai mask that we liked so much, or book a test drive with the same four-wheel car the show hosts are driving and much, much more. Mobile technology will find brand new and exciting applications.

.

Chapter 6

MORE DATA FOR EVERYBODY

6.1 **BIG DATA**

6.2 **BIG DATA** IN OUR EVERYDAY LIFE

6.3 **BUSINESSES** AND GOVERNMENTS, **TODAY**

6.4 **BIG DATA** FOR EVERYBODY

6.5 **LET'S PUT A CHECKMARK** ON OUR PRIVACY

6.1 BIG DATA

Allow me to start by debunking a myth: 'big data' doesn't mean 'many data'. Your 100,000-subscriber database may hold a lot of data, but they are not 'big data'. To make some big data out of them, you'll need to stop using your everyday life as a parameter, get to a higher level and start looking at things from above. You have to grow big, while all the rest stays small.

Big data are data that amount to a hundred petabytes, that is 1,000 billion gigabytes. Billions of USB keys.

CERN's Large Hadron Collider yields fifteen petabytes of data every year. It seems a lot but it's less data than a single person yields on the Internet in a single day. Also, big data are not only linked to online, digital or technological activities, but they include anything we can possibly log. For instance, try writing down your average walking day, including all the stops you make, the shop windows you look at, the people you meet. You'll get millions of data.

Some believe you can't do it. This is a lie: you only need some small sensors. After all, just like Industry 4.0 sensors allow us to calculate an object's life, from its manufacturing to its assembly and beyond, you can do pretty much the same with a person, or with all the people in a town.

Some already do. The automotive industry, for instance.

A study by McKinsey confirms that a last generation car, equipped with over 100 sensors feeding a constant flow of data, can log 25 gigabytes of data per hour. It's a humongous amount: a very big text file can be stored in under 2 megabytes.

If you consider that many of us drive their car to work, you'll see why cars are true data mines. And if you blend them with car owners...

Bingo! Here's your big data! They will hold the logs of their travels, but also the wear status of their tires, their accelerations, their turns, their mistakes when making a U-turn (resulting in a wealth of high quality information on their actual ability – or inability – to drive). Data become a precious source of information about who people really are when they're behind a wheel.

But there's so much more: what music do they listen to? Is it Bon Iver because they're hipsters? Or is it Leonard Cohen because they're politically active?

What route do they choose? Do they only drive on toll-free roads and are very careful about where they get their fuel fill? Well, even their parsimony is logged.

Your data may help your car manufacturer learn that you're not a good driver, or you're quite bad at steering or parking. The manufacturer may suggest you a professional driving course, which is a nice way of telling you: 'If you can't drive, I'll teach you'. But your data may be also used to give you a subtler suggestion, such as a special offer on parking sensors.

Safety should not be underestimated: according to the WHO, over one million people die in car accidents every year. If my car logs that when I drive at night I tend to swerve, I don't respect traffic laws, I don't stop at red lights or brake in an erratic way, police may be warned that something's wrong with me, or that I may have a drinking problem. Of course, there's a privacy issue, but after all this is about saving people's lives, so most citizens will most probably agree to put their privacy concerns aside.

In 2016, the 'connected car' market alone was worth 194 million dollars, but the value of big data that can be generated has already been deemed as 'virtually endless', incalculable. It's easy to imagine who may be interested in these data: repair shops would know how many spare tires they should stash in their warehouses, because they'd know who the bad drivers are.

I was running on empty on a highway once, but I got distracted and drove past the filling station. I immediatcly thought: 'If a refueling offer had been displayed as I was approaching the gas station, I'd have grasped it and it would have spared me this annoying experience'. Needless to say, such data are a godsend for automotive companies, while they allow consumers to save time and hassles. Some are sure that people will rise to defend data privacy, but I believe that only a minority will do.

The *2017 KPMG Global Automotive Executive Survey* shows that users are more inclined to hand over their power consumption and driving data than their personal data.

But aren't these personal data as well? Aren't the places I go and the way I reach them personal data?

ONLY A MINORITY WILL RISE TO DEFEND DATA PRIVACY

Of course they are, yet we don't realize.

It's not a matter of convenience: this is where the revolution is taking place.

If people were given something that makes their life easier, accelerates their jobs and allows them to save time, they would be ready to pay for it. Videogames such as Minecraft allow you to play and improve your gaming level, but it takes a lot of time and if you work till late you'll probably end up buying some game credits (with real money).

As Chris Anderson points out in his book *Free*,[23] once we used peer-to-peer systems to illegally download mp3 files for free, then came iTunes, which made us save a lot of time via a small adjustment in our mindset. Time is the discriminating factor for our future, and if giving away my data helps me save time and money, I will give them away with no hesitation.

Why should big data pertain to common people? Because they provide better services and help them have more time for themselves, so they can do the things they really like.

This aspect can't be underestimated anymore: people want free time, even if they use it to scroll through Facebook on the couch.

---

[23]Chris Anderson, *Free: The Future of a Radical Price*, New York, 2009

6.2 BIG DATA IN OUR EVERYDAY LIFE

If I feel sick and get hospitalized, a doctor turns me upside down, orders all appropriate tests, ponders the results and gives me a cure. If the cure doesn't work, she discusses my case with her colleagues. If their solution is ineffective, they start browsing their files and fat folders and see if they can find anything useful, or they turn on their computers and look up similar cases online or in specialized medical libraries.

Unfortunately, some will start from my symptoms and others from their hypotheses. I'll undergo more tests until they realize what's wrong with me (if I'm lucky). I'll be lying in my bed suffering, while they flip through their case studies to find a way to help me.

The doctors of the future will be nothing like today's: they'll be a machine that analyzes data.

Along with an AI system that can catalogue and organize such data, we'll be able to enter millions of records and obtain a data bank that can help doctors make their assessments. By looking up patients that show the same symptoms or off-kilter values as me, the system will pick any possible analogy and determine my problem. I know I'm oversimplifying: one of the limitations of current big data applications is the fact that data exist, they are everywhere, you can find them in whatever people do or write, but they're not easy to read. That's why we need experts who can do it.

However, we should stop envisioning one single individual who, like an old school analyst, devotes himself to reading billions of data to extract the most relevant results and sets up a strategy accordingly, like a doctor's who's treating a patient. It would be plain crazy. How long would it take to set things up and then write everything down?

Only machines and software can perform this task, with the result of simplifying and accelerating our activities.

According to IBM, their new Watson 'super computer' can store information from hundreds of scientific documents every day. This could mean that in a single day this cognitive learning system (a machine that learns from what we feed to it and can use data to perform new tasks) can complete a refresher course that a doctor averagely completes in one year or more. Will it replace doctors? It probably will, or at least it will dramatically shrink their number.

I read in the *New York Daily News*[24] that, in just ten minutes, Watson has

---

[24] 'New York Daily News', 1st May 2017 – BM's Watson gives proper diagnosis for Japanese leukemia patient after doctors were stumped for months - http://www.nydailynews.com/news/world/ibm-watson- proper-diagnosis-doctors-stumped-article-1.2741857

managed to complete a correct analysis of an old Japanese patient who suffered from a very peculiar variety of leukemia that had his doctors stumped for months. It may be corporate advertising, but a computer can obviously perform a high number of calculations and log quantities of information that a human being can't even imagine.

It's not just a matter of quality: actual savings will push everybody to accept the use of big data. Health prevention is improving and will keep on doing so using my data, which will be monitored daily and compared with other similar data. I will get a notification – remotely and with no doctors visiting me at home – if something's wrong, or if on a given day I should stay away from proteins or have my blood pressure checked.

The same applies to insurances. With a plethora of available data, possibly shared across multiple companies, predictive studies will be easier to make and companies will learn if I'm inclined to have a car accident, according to how I behave, what I do and what my driving habits are. This is where some concerns do arise, though, because I'm a techno music enthusiast: this means that I listen to it non-stop (in my car and anywhere else) and all my listening data are logged. But techno music lovers usually have a thing for fast driving, as they are carried away by the adrenalin rush this music gives them. This means my insurance agent needs to bypass the general cluster I'm included just because I listen to techno. I do not drive at break-neck speed because I listen to techno. Big data will allow my insurance company to single out my specific (and virtuous) driving habits, as we'll see, and this may even grant me a discount.

Some may object: 'What if my data show that I have some kind of physical anomaly or pathology and my health insurance fee is raised?' It is a political issue, indeed. Actually, this is an outstanding matter in USA, where the concept of 'pre-existing conditions' is often used to invalidate one's insurance coverage. Certainly, new laws need to be made. But, in order to do so, politicians will have to be proficient in such issues. Big data mainly include 'raw' data, pieces of information that need further codification before they can be used to split an audience into clusters. For instance, data about people strolling inside a shopping mall do not give any indication on who they are, but by processing all available data you could trace some movement 'maps'. You could single out a specific point that corresponds to a specific individual by using the data about his purchases or the loyalty card he's used or enabled on that very day.

Today's technology already allows us to do this, and it would be crazy not to take full advantage of big data. We'll soon get used to being 'cuddled' and pampered by obtaining the services and things we love in the shortest possible time. And if this implies giving up some of our privacy, we'll be happy to oblige.

6.3 BUSINESSES AND GOVERNMENTS, TODAY

There's one role that future companies and agencies will require: a data analyst, a profile that's still rather unknown in Italy. Every month, some new research confirms that about 10, 20 or 30,000 data analysts are wanted by companies. I always find figures risky, because sometimes parents use them to push their children to pick jobs they have no talent for. My advice is you shouldn't even think about data analysis if you don't love statistics and calculations. And as for companies: it's not easy to find such roles. Data analysts are very few and the good ones are hard to win over, not to mention that they cost a lot (in some fields quality still matters, you know). These people are true geeks, they get excited at scrolling numbers, algorithms and functions.

Just forget the yuppie type, data analysts are more the lab mouse type.

There are very few data analysts around the world and they're extremely rare in Italy. Our country is struggling and not really trying to compensate, despite all the claims. Trying to stop the future is like Don Quixote assaulting a windmill; the wheel will simply keep on turning, silently, and the poor knight of conservatorism will end up unsaddled and beaten.

According to McKinsey, the use of big data can increase the operational margins of businesses up to 60%. Even if it was it 40% or 30%, why wouldn't an entrepreneur invest in such a favorable technology? I'm sure some still wouldn't, as the world is full of backward-looking people, but they'd soon be replaced by younger and Industry 4.0-oriented entrepreneurs. According to a Gartner research, 75% of enterprises will soon invest in big data to improve their customer experience (which is a priority for two businesses out of three) and enhance their marketing activities.

However, we have to go beyond the simple customer experience we're used to (a customer buys a product and the product is improved according to the customer's needs). Located in the eastern hinterland of Milan, the Segrate-Pioltello area is a new residential district that is being developed as a 'smart city'. Smart cities are places where sensors and other instruments monitor the consumption of water, power, gas and much more in order to provide a better service to citizens and save money and resources. In this case, the real breakthrough is that data will be sold and proceedings will be invested in welfare services.

Data for sale are very interesting for companies, but the possibility of reusing earnings for a community is certainly as interesting.

It's a great challenge for the EU, which enforces a public and transparent control over many collected data, while there's no such a strict right to privacy in the USA, where data are much easier to collect and sell.

This is the opposite of what happens in the ultimate 'smart city', Singapore (which we've already covered): here everything is controlled by central computers, from traffic to people's lives. Not only the system can recognize the number of underground train passengers according to the different times of day, but it can even track single individuals along their route. By calculating all passengers' routes, the system can suggest how schedules can be adjusted in order to prevent queues, overcrowded stations and empty train cars.

There's also a special street traffic system that would make Italians crazy: it's based on electronic billboards that prevent cars from accessing jammed streets and force them to take alternate, longer routes.

There's no human operator determining which streets must be blocked: an algorithm does that. If you drive through a blocked road, you'll get a 30+ dollar fine.

All citizens own a smart card logging everything, from their routes to their violations. What about privacy? Well, they all know that everything is being traced.

If you need to make a negotiation with a Singapore citizen, you can ask the government the permission to access part of their data. In the end, a person's value is their reputation, because the people here are wealthy enough to afford their individual freedom to be put aside and fines do no impact them much. Also, in this area of the Asian world the value of freedom is much different from Europe. Control is always welcome, provided you get order in return.

Technology and data help things work, big data are collected to anticipate people's needs.

A mega computer accumulates and continuously analyzes everything, using algorithms that replace the government. I believe that this would never work in Europe: we think differently, we have a huge and long-standing love for freedom and we even need to unleash our anarchic side every now and then. In Singapore, a non-authorized demonstration would be harshly shut off, with arrests and the occasional death sentence.

During an interview on Italian television (*Speciale Tg1*, 29th January 2017), Crystal Albidin, one the world's most famous young anthropologists, claimed that Singapore has managed to unite ethnicities, but at the cost of transparency. In other words, nobody knows who's in charge of control and why, nor what the rules are; this way, 'free will' activists can do nothing.

If bus drivers are slow and don't stick to their schedules, they don't get paid. If this happened in Rome, bus drivers would indefinitely paralyze the city with strikes. In Singapore you'll find YouTubers appointed by the government to promote 'positive' activities among young people or women.

Singapore may be the 'Country of Control,' but I bet that people from Milan or San Francisco would love faster transports that allow them to save time when they go to work. Sure, punishing late bus drivers sounds like Soviet Union, but then again the last time I went to Rome I waited for about 25 minutes for a bus that was so overcrowded (a livestock car!) that I had to catch a taxi anyway. In conclusion, I want neither unbearably strict rules nor total chaos.

In Stockholm, 1,600 special GPS trackers were installed on taxi cabs to monitor traffic and decongest the city. It was a successful idea, as the average travel times were reduced by 50% and air pollution experienced a 10% decrease.

I'm not shocked at these figures and I'm pretty sure anyone will appreciate them. Also, by using taxis, which are public service vehicles, private citizens are not bothered and their privacy isn't invaded, even if they want to make a detour to their local red light district. No system would log that.

However, in Europe freedom is still considered an essential value. What will ordinary people do with data? Probably nothing, but you could spend days scrolling numbers and statistics on the *European Open Data Portal*, from education to science. It's a tool for transparency, even if most collected data somehow make their way to the USA.

6.4 BIG DATA FOR EVERYBODY

According to a wild and untraceable prejudice, big data are only efficient for big companies. Funny as it may sound, this is actually a tragedy for my country. We spend most of our time claiming that SMEs are the foundation of Italian economy, and in time of elections politicians even flirt with crafts associations to get their votes. However, when a true revolution like big data comes, we deem it as unsuitable for our economic system. By pushing themselves into a corner, Italians tell the world they can't keep up with their pace and future.

So let me state this clearly: big data are within everybody's reach, both big and small enterprises.

The only difference lies in quantity: while big companies need a bigger amount of data, small companies have to rely on less details.

Focusing on theory makes us miss the point, I'm afraid: we must learn to analyze and use information, and turn raw and unorganized data into contents that can be studied. We need to be able to use them by setting up a proper framework and by hiring people who can perform some true data-driven management, the kind that allows a business to take real actions based on numbers and their insights.

We should be betting on data scientists. Big companies must have internal teams with statistics experts who can also blend figures and social studies. Small companies can rely on third party firms or they can join together, create a network and cut down technology costs. Today's expensive tools will most probably be affordable for all of them in the near future.

If companies don't invest now, they will only achieve one result: going out of the market.

Right now, the use of big data can improve two factors: the operation of business tasks – though this has more to do with Industry 4.0 – and marketing. A company wants to learn as much as possible about an individual, because the resulting data can be used to set up tailored marketing activities. This way, a company can make targeted advertisements for a 'perfect' product and avoid shooting in the dark. An example: my Facebook feed keeps on showing me SUV ads, despite the fact I don't like them at all. This means that a lot of money is being wasted: despite the amount of data he can collect, Mr. Zuckerberg cannot target me properly. This is not different from Amazon offers relying on the 'Those who bought this product, also bought these' model.

We are fed many useful suggestions (a nice reflex camera is often shown with matching lens), but also a lot of stuff that won't suit us. We're included in a cluster and deemed as in line with the majority of our 'counterparts', but the truth is that people don't necessarily think alike and I may prefer white products over black products. No harm done, sure, I'll look for something white. But if a white object doesn't spontaneously come to my mind, I won't look for it and won't buy it. Had it been suggested to me on my Amazon page, I'd have probably purchased it right away.

Yes, the future will require cross-referencing offline data with online data. It's something companies already do in America: they buy a consumer's email address and, by applying psychology to marketing, they can – or at least successfully try to – determine what that specific consumer likes.

I'm not talking about a database with a dozen thousand contacts, though: I'm talking about blending billions of data.

Humans are predictable creatures, they are social animals. In one of his most interesting experiments, Massachusetts Institute of Technology professor Alex Pentland[25] recounts monitoring the movements of a large number of students inside a university campus. Before the

---

[25] For more information, see his book 'Social Physics. How Social Networks Can Makes Us Smarter', Penguin, New York 2014

elections, their social divisions would hugely increase, with Democrats only attending some bars and clubs and Republicans attending others. Don't we all think this usually happens? Of course we do, but Pentland actually collected such data using the chips installed on the students' mobile phones. Via a set of social experiments, he demonstrated that being exposed to external influences actually conditions our behaviors. If we can learn about these behaviors, we'll be able to foretell each individual's voting intentions. This is no small business: data allow you to learn about a single individual's ideas, not his reference cluster's or group's. From a marketing perspective, this ability gives you a whole wealth of opportunities.

So far, analysts have dealt with so-called 'sentiments' on social platforms, an ongoing analysis of tweets and posts that is supposed to tell what our society will do. This approach may work for a limited number of analyses, but in most cases it simply doesn't, even though newspapers love to put so much emphasis on these calculations. After Trump's election in 2016, a research center claimed they had predicted his victory on Twitter, but their prediction actually showed a 65%-35% range and almost all States being pro-Trump, while in reality he even lost on popular votes. On a technical basis, this survey's results were totally wrong (15% is a huge difference), but the commentator was thrilled nonetheless. A perfect example of random numbers passed off as accurate predictions.

Using a citizen's movements we will also be able to predict her preferences as a consumer, or her financial risks, and so on. Pentland conducted a research about this, as well. Smart cities such as Singapore are quite famous, but Pentland is not favorable to such control systems. But his study pertains the improvement of what a city's life is impacted by, such as power consumption, traffic, war on crime or the spreading of diseases. Pentland's analysis identifies each individual's daily travels for work and family reasons or shopping purposes, even during weekends and holidays, and can single out what they like to do.

Such data are important for both social and corporate purposes. If I worked for the government, I'd strongly rely on them, because they'd allow me to improve people's lives, resolve traffic issues, help the war on crime by expanding social networks. In other words, big data could be a true boon for politics.

For instance, environmental scientists increasingly account for IoT-oriented technologies and the smart use of big data for the development of 'high precision agriculture'. Using sensors and researches, they aim at having a set of real-time data – about weather, soil quality, parasites and so on – allowing them to act both in real time

and via loss- and cost-reducing long-term strategies. These data cou
be useful, for instance, for notifying farmers when they should refrain
from irrigating because heavy showers are coming.

Speaking of big data, Food LogiQ, a software firm promoting food safety
via traceability and sustainability, has developed a system that stores a
product's data at each stage of the supply and transport chains and
thus allows food businesses to prevent contamination, to accurately
select the goods that need disposal and to avoid the useless waste of
full batches.

Experts are also performing real-time monitoring of climate variations
using sensors scattered across the world, especially at the planet's
poles, to help fight climate change.

I believe that companies should take advantage of data for their sales as
well: if a consumer likes a product because he always goes shopping at
the same place, the manufacturer should be able to display it in the best
possible way.

Or if a user always drives along the same route, he may be offered the
best Uber or car sharing deal for that route.

**The development of such data will necessarily be a driver for
marketing automation.** Data analysts can't be working on billions of
data all day; companies would need thousands of them, who would

react with a predictable lag anyway.

Programmed algorithms will come in handy, as they can adapt to changes in real time. And artificial intelligence will, as well.

After a 'long cold winter', we're now back to discussing AI outside of robotics labs or Hollywood movies. It's finally being considered for marketing purposes. In general, the excitement for big data, even from titans such as Google and Facebook, has pushed many businesses to heavily invest in data collection, storage and organization, taking AI out of its hibernation and accelerating its integration.

According to a research by eMarketer,[26] in coming years the use of AI will dramatically accelerate and play an increasingly leading role in 3D printing (+78%), self-driving vehicles (+63%) and chatbots (+22%). Artificial intelligence and big data will make us rethink products as well: the world giant of insurance software, Majesco, has partnered with IBM to use Watson's cognitive computing to use predictive data as a basic tool to develop new consumer services and products.

The main concern is still how well we know these tools: according to a report by 'Narrative Science', **88% of managers working at companies owning AI applications claim they've never used them**, but the truth is that they actually make a daily use of applications such

---

[26] 'Artificial Intelligence 2016: What's Now, What's New and What's Next'

as virtual personal assistants, which integrate AI. I call it a paradox when a boss doesn't know what tools he's got.

And speaking of tools, the only way to properly handle big data (whether they are profiled or not) is via a DMP, a Data Management Platform. Many readers will probably know about it, but here's a quick refresher. A DMP is a 'super software' combining data processing applications and audience monitoring programs.

As we discussed above, DMPs are still quite expensive, but it's just a matter of time before they become affordable for a larger audience. Meanwhile, small companies could get together, outsource this task to a third party and share expenses.

Day after day, these tools are improving their user-profiling skills: they aggregate a user's online activity (logged by cookie files) and his offline data extracted from a database of past purchases (which leverages email addresses and phone numbers), phone contacts, car sharing travels and much more. Some companies are also including activities that include vouchers and discounts, since people tend to more lightheartedly give their data when benefits and savings are involved. Despite this, a perfect algorithm that can understand exactly who I am still needs to be invented.

An interesting theory is becoming popular and it's related to a discipline called psychometrics. Former Cambridge and currently Stanford professor Michal Kosinski has allegedly developed a method for guessing people's preferences and traits from their Facebook 'Likes'. Kosinski has demonstrated that 68 'Likes' allow him to learn a person's skin color (with a 95% accuracy), sexual orientation, political stance. By increasing the number of monitored 'Likes', he can tell an individual's religious belief, history of drugs/alcohol abuse and so on. With 300 'Likes' he'll know somebody better than his/her partner. According to Kosinski, we could get to know a man's preferences better than he does, just as social psychoanalysis does.

Let's not delve into whether he's right or not, as this studies are still at an experimental stage, but Kosinski's name has made the headlines after Trump's election, because a company called Cambridge Analytica bragged about having used psychometrics to monitor single electors and convince them to vote for the tycoon. Actually, many journalists have already objected that Cambridge Analytica may simply be doing branding campaigns at Republican conventions to win some new customers. Some reporters point out that the company has simply bought user data for profiling purposes in a political campaign. For instance, Cambridge Analytica determined the most purchased products in the Haiti and Miami areas, bought their purchasers' email addresses and flooded them with Facebook ads about the Clinton Foundation allegedly wasting the money allocated for post-quake reconstructions in Haiti.[27]

What is the truth and what is propaganda? I can't tell. But I can confirm that this is not impossible to make, at least when it comes to cross-referencing databases, and that psychometrics theories are realistic. If you think about it, American car dealers can sell the contact details of those who bought a car. If politics can already efficiently use data, companies shouldn't be caught off guard.

---

[27] The Data That Turned the World Upside Down –
https://motherboard.vice.com/en_us/article/how-our- likes-helped-trump-win, 1st June 2017.

6.5 LET'S PUT A CHECKMARK ON OUR PRIVACY

On 10th September 2013, Americans were preparing to commemorate the twelfth anniversary of the greatest tragedy in their recent history, a one-of-a-kind media event that was so unique that it sparkled two major aspects in terms of modernity.

One is taking its name from a date. '9/11' has become a dictionary word, a figure of speech, it has turned into actual substance. In doing so, it has also occupied a box in our calendars forever, because we know that there will never be another 9/11 like in 2001.

The other factor is interesting from a sociological and behavioral perspective: 9/11 is the only point in time for which all citizens of the Western world can exactly remember where they were and with whom. 'We shall not forget', we write and promise. We *could never* forget in this case.

But let's get back to 10th September 2013.

4,756 kilometers from Ground Zero, at Town Hall conference center in Cupertino, California, Apple's chairman Tim Cook activated his iPhone 5C screen using his fingerprint.

A cool and hot technology, an amazing design, a sense of proximity and empathy. But as a matter of fact, the potential creation of the greatest fingerprint archive on Earth.

Fingerprints are not being shared by Apple, of course, and they stay on our iPhones. And the company is very serious about protecting their customers' privacy, even when they're criminals.

But our concern is real. What if a secret cloud exists? Or a very skilled hacker? A delusional Apple engineer?

Four years and a billion users later (and all their fingerprints stored in their iPhones) Mr. Cook was back with a new magic trick.

In 2017, the day after the 9/11 commemoration, he launched iPhone X, which:

1) Costs 1,200 dollars, just like a laborer's monthly salary or ten tattoos;

2) Is all made with glass, on both sides. It features no buttons. You could say it's all surface;

3) Is not activated by fingerprints, but a face recognition technology. It can tell your face from mine and the billions of other faces that will most probably use this technology in the next four years.

What about your concerns for a secret cloud or an evil hacker now? Well, mine are growing.

There's two more considerations I'd like to add:

1) Something new will come in four years, launched right after 9/11 as per Apple's tradition. My prediction? DNA. iPhone Y will recognize the cells on a user's hand. This addition counts up to a billion fingerprints, a billion faces and a billion sequences of deoxyribonucleic acid;

2) People are media, always, anywhere and most of all here. Our fingerprints and our faces will be at the mercy of secret clouds and evil hackers. And we'll have paid 1,200 Euros to allow this.

Conclusions

LEARN, EVERY DAY

We may be wrong about
many things,
but we're damn sure about
one:
the digital age has only
begun.

We're two professionals. We've been doing our jobs for 25 years, amounting to about 9,000 days. For 9,000 days we've seen things come and go, and used them all: 'brand new' objects, devices and work tools such as pocket calculators, modems, pizza or sushi deliveries during office meetings, green phosphor monitors, programming languages, water bowl dispensers with plastic cups.

Every single day we've made decisions, we've allowed our employees their holidays, we've granted performance bonuses. We may have failed or lost a client or two along the way, but we've also made some great achievements.

Every single day we've learned something.

If you work for 9,000 days, you end up learning 9,000 different things.

We may be wrong about many of them, but we're damn sure about one: the digital age has only begun.

Just like it took us thousands of years to begin fusing metal after we discovered fire, we'll need years, maybe decades, to see technology work like we want it to.

Streaming a TV series on a mobile phone and making a high-quality video call with a friend in Australia aren't technological innovations, nor are our 'Likes', posts, clicks, searches, retweets or the thrilling moment Google wishes us happy birthday on our exact birthday.

These are only doses, pills. Or fodder, if you prefer a more bucolic analogy.

The companies we interact with are fattening us up to get something out of us. A heap of well-organized bits from which they can obtain what they need in order to operate their business.

We're cookies, lookalikes, synopses, heatmaps, a/b tests. We're targets. And we know what being a target means in a war.

Luckily there's no war, not yet. We're still the ones in charge, and this new era is still firmly in our hands.

Until recently, Italian television was monitored by Auditel, the audience rating service. The two main channels, Rai 1 and Canale 5, would rage on with extremely high ratings. Advertising was a true business driver and you had to pay big money to be on TV, because being on TV could change people's behaviors. And sell products.

Today, the effectiveness of communication is both more solid and aleatory. A message gets increasingly refined but also deteriorates as it reaches much narrower targets, and it often ends up drifting in the communication ocean we're all exposed to every day (about 5,000 messages a day, some say).

We live liquid lives, we receive slippery, 'soaped up' messages that ceaselessly brush past us and never actually surprise us, touch us, change our behaviors.

Propagation techniques become increasingly sophisticated, their methods and contents changing with our location and our disposition to receive advertising messages.

In the morning, we're commuters who love to swipe through our social profiles. We get lost in all those Instagram pictures and Facebook videos.

It doesn't (hopefully) happen while we drive, in which case we listen to the radio. And here's one of the secrets behind a brand's success: a strategic medium. Chasing people using the right tools isn't enough anymore, though. The 'soap up' effect is just around the corner. We speak, but hardly anyone listens. We're constantly distracted, and skip from one distraction to the next. So what can we do? What is a brand's role, and what is the task of those in charge of selling it in the era of selfies, Facebook kitten pictures and YouTubers?

If the next playing field is not a prime time TV show, but a Candy Crush game, how can a brand compete and catch our attention?

The future of digital communication depends on two key factors. One is about companies and brands and it's called 'storytelling'. It's the ability to convey a message as a story that is relevant to a user, with a low cost and a high dissemination potential.

The other factor is about people and it's the way a message's relevance can, even for just one second, make somebody perform an action. A picture, a 'Like', a share, a comment.

People's actions propagate to the sounding board of their contacts. It's like a GRP, a gross rating point. People are a brand new medium.

As simplicistic as it may seem (but also quite exhaustive, since ours are very simple times), we could say that the outcome of a message could be calculated as follows:

$$success = [quality\ of\ a\ story]\ x\ [dissemination\ multiplier].$$

When we look at our children, we find them so different from us at their age, and it's because they really *are* different. Those who were born after 1995 take the Internet for granted and have native digital behaviors.

It's not only a matter of looking up the news on the Internet or being extremely familiar with social networks. It means they're authentically accustomed to 'real time' dynamics, the 'here and now', the unrepeatable moment.

It means they know how to celebrate that moment the proper way, calibrating the weight of a comment, a 'Like' or a share according to their interlocutor, the time of day and the unavoidable personal allusions that are inherent to each of these specific online actions.

It means they can take the right 'micro-decision' at the right time and enforce it, immediately before the post they're interacting with is flooded by an infinite discussion thread.

It means they enjoy music using playlists, skipping from one track to the other, totally ignoring the concept of an album.

It means they fight tooth and nail for an instant of celebrity, or their 'fifteen seconds of fame' as a modern-day Andy Warhol would put it.

It means they don't know how to get bored anymore. If their Internet connection fails for two hours, they keep refreshing a page instead of doing something else until the connection is back.

The digital era has profoundly affected their lives and deeply changed ours.

Our awareness of having a smartphone in our pockets, which has become an all-encompassing device, and of having a social profile, which has become a biased billboard that only shows things we care for *(echo chamber)*, has distorted our roles in history.

We believe we can really make a difference now, we believe we can count, and that's simply because we can tweet one of the Prime

Minister's interns or put up a fight with people who don't share our opinion about a shallow detail, eventually wishing each other some horrible death. We believe we can seduce a beautiful woman who's amazingly attracted to us, but prefer to ignore that most probably she's just a click-baiting bot or a truck driver from Iowa mocking us. So-called 'bottom-up democracies' have discarded some values, culture above all, making us believe that voting for a major reform and posting a picture of our dog or our new tattoo are essentially the same thing.

So here we are, look at us: fragile and lonely at our browsers. Unable to concentrate on what we were looking up in the first place, preys to links that must be clicked and to a *stream of consciousness* that carries us away, we spend hours toggling from a football video to an article about a murder in Belgium.

Our browser is where we can find ourselves. Our cache memory is the flight recorder of our digital lives. It stores the pictures of the holidays we wish we had made, the car fittings we dream we could afford and the names of the people we have looked up on Facebook.

We've learned that in the best case scenario digital technology has irreversibly changed our lives and a set of behaviors that seemed deeply rooted. We can now have our custom pizza delivered at our address while we're still on the train.

We can have the best products, always, at the best price. Or at least we can believe it is so.

We can deceive ourselves and believe that, when people look at the best version of ourselves, the one we carefully choose to showcase, they'll envy or want us. We can try and believe that our opinions on Facebook will remain forever, carved in digital stone. Therefore we post an epitaph every day, or a precious aphorism.

All of this will come to an end, obviously.

That's when we'll stop feeling guilty if we get bored or disappoint ourselves, or when we feel mediocre for a minute. **That's when we'll finally be able to start using technology to improve the world, and ourselves.**

Special thanks

Silvio and Aldo would like to thank:

Mondadori and in particular Stefano Peccatori and Virginia Ponciroli.
Marco Montemagno for his preface.
Massimo Capucci for the book title and Luca Fulciniti for the cover.

People are media is dedicated to our families.

Graphic design

Cristina Menotti

English translation

[placeholder], Milano

Made in the USA
Lexington, KY
05 September 2018